Nuclear Energy: Friend or Foe?

Examining Nuclear Power Issues from a Systems Perspective

Second Edition

A Problem-Based Unit Designed
for 6th–8th Grade Learners

KENDALL/HUNT PUBLISHING COMPANY
4050 Westmark Drive   Dubuque, Iowa 52002

Book Team
Chairman and Chief Executive Officer: *Mark C. Falb*
President and Chief Operating Officer: *Chad M. Chandlee*
Director of National Book Program: *Paul B. Carty*
Editorial Development Manager: *Georgia Botsford*
Developmental Editor: *Lynnette M. Rogers*
Vice President, Operations: *Timothy J. Beitzel*
Assistant Vice President, Production Services: *Christine E. O'Brien*
Senior Production Editor: *Charmayne McMurray*
Permissions Editor: *Renae Horstman*
Cover Designer: *Jenifer Chapman*

Author Information for Correspondence and Workshops:
Center for Gifted Education
The College of William and Mary
P.O. Box 8795
Williamsburg, VA 23187-8795
Phone: 757-221-2362
Email address: *cfge@wm.edu*
Web address: *www.cfge.wm.edu*

**Center for Gifted Education Staff,
First Edition**
Project Director: Dr. Joyce VanTassel-Baska
Project Managers: Dr. Shelagh A. Gallagher
Dr. Victoria B. Damiani
Project Consultants: Dr. Beverly T. Sher
Linda Neal Boyce
Dana T. Johnson
Dr. Jill D. Burruss
Dennis R. Hall
Teacher Developer: Rebecca F. Crossett

**Center for Gifted Education Staff,
Second Edition**
Executive Director: Dr. Joyce VanTassel-Baska
Director: Dr. Elissa F. Brown
Curriculum Director and Unit Editor: Dr. Kimberley L. Chandler
Curriculum Writers: Dr. Janice I. Robbins
Brandy L. Evans
Dr. Kimberley L. Chandler
Curriculum Reviewer: Dr. Beverly T. Sher

The William and Mary Center for Gifted Education logo is a depiction of the Crim Dell Bridge, a popular site on the William and Mary campus. Since 1964, this Asian-inspired structure has been a place for quiet reflection as well as social connections. The bridge represents the goals of the Center for Gifted Education: to link theory and practice, to connect gifted students to effective learning experiences, to offer career pathways for graduate students, and to bridge the span between general education and the education of gifted learners.

Cover and Part Opener Image © Galen Rowell/Corbis.
This unit was previously titled **Hot Rods.**

Contents

Introduction

Unit Introduction

Nuclear Energy: Friend or Foe? is a problem-based science unit designed for high-ability learners in the middle grades. Elements of the unit have been successfully used with all learners in a wide variety of situations, from pullout programs for gifted learners to traditional heterogeneously grouped classrooms. The unit allows middle-school students to explore a variety of systems in a novel way, namely, through the process of grappling with an ill-structured, real-world problem.

Because the unit is problem-based, the way in which a teacher implements the unit will necessarily differ from the way in which most traditional science units are taught. Preparing for and implementing problem-based learning takes time, flexibility, and a willingness to experiment with a new way of teaching.

The total time required for completion of *Nuclear Energy: Friend or Foe?* should be minimally 50 hours, with more time required for additional activities.

Rationale

This unit has been designed to introduce or reinforce the overarching science concept of systems in an engaging fashion. The problem-based learning format was chosen in order to allow students to acquire significant science content knowledge in the course of solving an interdisciplinary, real-world problem. This format requires students to analyze the problem situation, determine what information they need in order to generate potential solutions, and then find that information in a variety of ways. In addition to library work and other information-gathering methods, students, with teacher facilitation, perform experiments of their own design in order to find information necessary to derive and evaluate solutions to the problem. The problem-based method also allows students to model the scientific process, from the problem-finding and information-gathering steps to the evaluation of experimental data and the recasting or solution of the problem. Finally, the overarching scientific concept of systems provides students with a framework for the analysis of both their experiments and the problem as a whole.

A variety of systems, including nuclear power plant systems and social systems, are presented in the context of a simulated real-world problem. The need to develop a resolution for this unit problem motivates student interest. Through the problem-based process, students will acquire significant science content knowledge in areas such as nuclear physics and biology. They will also model the scientific process in their search for information necessary for the resolution of the problem. This information will be obtained not only from books and other traditional resource materials but also from hands-on experimentation and from outside resource people, including practicing scientists.

Implementation Time

The total time that is required for completion of *Nuclear Energy: Friend or Foe?* is a minimum of 50 hours, with more time required for additional lessons.

Assessment

Nuclear Energy: Friend or Foe? contains many assessment opportunities that can be used to monitor student progress and assess student learning. Opportunities for formative assessment include the following:

- The student's **Problem Log** is a written compilation of the student's thoughts about the problem. Most lessons contain suggested questions for students to answer in their **Problem Logs.** The **Problem Log** should also be used by the student to record and store data and new information that he or she has obtained during the course of the unit.
- Other metacognitive forms are used to help the student explain his or her solutions to particular parts of the problem.
- Teacher observation of student participation in large- and small-group activities is another opportunity for ongoing assessment.

Opportunities for summative assessment include the following:

- The final resolution activity involves a small-group presentation of a solution for the unit's ill-structured problem. The quality of the solution will reflect the group's understanding of the science involved as well as the societal and ethical considerations needed to form an acceptable solution.
- Final post-assessments allow the teacher to determine whether individual students have met the systems objectives, science content, and science process skills listed in the Curriculum Framework at the beginning of the unit.

Appendix E, Suggested Rubrics, includes suggestions for assessing experimental design process skills, connections to the systems concept, oral presentations, and persuasive writing.

New to This Edition

Student books are available for purchase to provide students an opportunity to record information about the problems as they progress through the units.

Included in the student books are the Problem Log Questions, Student Brainstorming Guides, Experimental Design Diagrams, Student Experimental Protocols, and Student Laboratory Reports, along with the Glossary and Laboratory Safety Precautions.

The books are designed to be consumable.

Words to the Wise Teacher:

The unit you are about to begin, *Nuclear Energy: Friend or Foe?*, consists of 22 lessons; the unit requires a minimum of 50 hours of instruction. A letter for parents is included that you may wish to send home with your students or use as a template for your own letter to be distributed before beginning the unit. The letter describes the goals of the curriculum as well as ways parents can supplement the unit at home.

The unit includes many opportunities for students to participate actively in solving a real-world problem. Some of these activities involve homework that supplements class work; others involve research conducted in a library/media center or online. Please read the unit before beginning to teach so that you have a sense of when you might need materials and assistance from your media specialist.

Handouts for the unit are included, as well as some background information on various topics. A separate notebook or Problem Log is required for each student. A materials list at the beginning of each lesson notes specific items for that lesson; however, you may wish to procure additional items depending upon the need for students to probe some concepts more in-depth or to design additional experiments.

Several methods for assessing student progress are indicated in the unit. Assessments ask students to demonstrate understanding of the unit concept within the relevant context. Writing activities will include essays, a research project, and Problem Log responses throughout the unit. Finally, post-assessments are included that may be used to compare student achievement at the conclusion of the unit to their knowledge at the beginning.

A section providing some implementation guidelines and the key teaching models of the unit follows the lesson plans. Teachers are encouraged to read this section and, if possible, to attend an implementation workshop about the units. Contact the Center for Gifted Education for more information.

The Center for Gifted Education thanks you for your interest in our materials!

Alignment to National Science Education Standards and Benchmarks for Science Literacy

Category of Standard	Nuclear Energy: Friend or Foe?	National Science Education Standards	Benchmarks for Science Literacy
Concept	Students will be able to: 1. Analyze systems; 2. Use systems language; 3. Analyze systems interactions; 4. Make predictions based on systems thinking; and 5. Transfer systems concept to new systems.	A system is an organized group of related objects or components that form a whole. Systems have boundaries, components, resource flow (input and output) and feedback. The goal of this standard is to think and analyze in terms of systems. Prediction is the use of knowledge to identify and explain observations or changes in advance.	Systems: 1. A system is something that consists of many parts; the parts usually influence one another. 2. A system may not work as well if a part of it is missing, broken, worn out, mismatched, or misconnected.
Content/ Topics	Students will be able to: 1. Describe events that occur during the process of nuclear fission and nuclear fusion; 2. Explain the effect of the products of nuclear fission on the environment; 3. Understand where and how nuclear fission occurs within a nuclear power plant; 4. Evaluate the effects of radiation on daily life; 5. Model and graph the process of radioactive decay; 6. Evaluate the curve of a graph that models radioactive decay; 7. Infer the benefits or detriments to industries that produce low-level radioactive waste; 8. Discover and appreciate the problems inherent in storing high-level radioactive waste; 9. Reason about situations or events that require attention to nuclear safety; 10. Describe the uses of shielding materials, both for nuclear power plants and for other applications;	Physical Science: 1. Students will develop the understanding of properties of objects and materials. Science in Personal and Social Perspectives: 2. Students will develop an understanding of science and technology in local challenges.	Nature of Mathematics: 1. Mathematical ideas can be expressed graphically. Technology & Science: 2. Measuring instruments can be used to gather accurate scientific comparisons. Structure of Matter: 3. When a new material is made by combining two or more materials, it has different properties.

continued

Category of Standard	Nuclear Energy: Friend or Foe?	National Science Education Standards	Benchmarks for Science Literacy
Content/ Topics (Cont.)	11. Investigate the shielding properties of various materials for a safe form of electromagnetic radiation, either visible or ultraviolet light; 12. Describe the problem of storage of nuclear waste and discuss the relative merits and deficiencies of various solutions to this problem; 13. Evaluate the relative risks of nuclear power and of other power-generation methods, both to nearby consumers and to future generations; 14. Research an area of choice within the field of nuclear energy; and 15. Communicate understanding of newly acquired information to others.		
Scientific Processes	Students will be able to: 1. Design, perform, and report on the results of experiments; 2. Demonstrate data handling; 3. Analyze experimental data; 4. Make predictions to similar problems; 5. Communicate understanding to others; and 6. Identify meaningful scientific problems for investigation.	Students will be able to: 1. Ask a question about objects, organisms, and events in the environment; 2. Plan and conduct a simple investigation; 3. Employ simple equipment and tools to gather data and extend the senses; 4. Use data to construct a reasonable explanation; and 5. Communicate investigations and explanations.	Students should know that: 1. Scientific investigations may take many different forms; 2. Results of similar investigations seldom turn out the same; 3. Scientists' explanations come from observation and thinking; 4. Claims must be backed up with evidence; and 5. Clear communication is an essential part of doing science.

Nuclear Energy: Friend or Foe?
Curriculum Goals

1. Concept	2. Content
Goal 1: To develop understanding of the concept of systems and of the structure, function, and pattern of key systems elements	**Goal 2:** To understand the principles of fusion and fission and the effect of their products on the environment

Curriculum Outcomes

Students will be able to

1. Analyze a problem system and certain systems related to nuclear energy;
2. Articulate in oral and written form how and why systems work using appropriate systems language such as *boundaries, elements, input, and output;*
3. Demonstrate how given systems interact with each other (e.g. both real world and experimental);
4. Predict the impact of multiple solutions to the given problem within each system;
5. Generalize systems knowledge across problems;
6. Assess how human systems change over time based on needs, resources, and circumstances.

Students will be able to

1. Describe events that occur during the process of nuclear fission and nuclear fusion;
2. Explain the effect of the products of nuclear fission on the environment;
3. Understand where and how nuclear fission occurs within a nuclear power plant;
4. Evaluate the effects of radiation on daily life;
5. Model and graph the process of radioactive decay;
6. Evaluate the curve of a graph that models radioactive decay;
7. Infer the benefits or detriments to industries that produce low-level radioactive waste;
8. Discover and appreciate the problems inherent in storing high-level radioactive waste;
9. Reason about situations or events that require attention to nuclear safety;
10. Describe the uses of shielding materials, both for nuclear power plants and for other applications;
11. Investigate the shielding properties of various materials for a safe form of electromagnetic radiation, either visible or ultraviolet light;
12. Describe the problem of storage of nuclear waste and discuss the relative merits and deficiencies of various solutions to this problem;
13. Evaluate the relative risks of nuclear power and of other power-generation methods, both to nearby consumers and to future generations;
14. Research an area of choice within the field of nuclear energy;
15. Communicate understanding of newly acquired information to others.

3. Process/Expermental Design	4. Process/Reasoning
Goal 3: To understand and apply the principles of basic experimental design	**Goal 4:** To develop reasoning skills with application to science

Curriculum Outcomes

Students will be able to

1. Design, perform, and report on the results of experiments related to a given problem;
2. Demonstrate good data-handling skills;
3. Analyze experimental data as appropriate;
4. Evaluate experimental results;
5. Transfer knowledge to make predictions about similar problems;
6. Articulate enhanced understanding of the scientific area to others.

Students will be able to

1. Define a problem, given ill-structured, complex, or technical information;
2. Formulate multiple perspectives (at least two) on a given issue;
3. State assumptions behind a line of reasoning;
4. Apply science concepts appropriately;
5. Provide evidence and data to support a claim, issue, or thesis statement;
6. Make inferences, based on evidence;
7. Draw implications for action based on the available data.

Lesson Organizational Chart

This chart is a graphic depiction of the curriculum framework as it is incorporated within the lesson plans. Each lesson is listed under the heading of the primary type of goal that is covered (concept, content, or process).

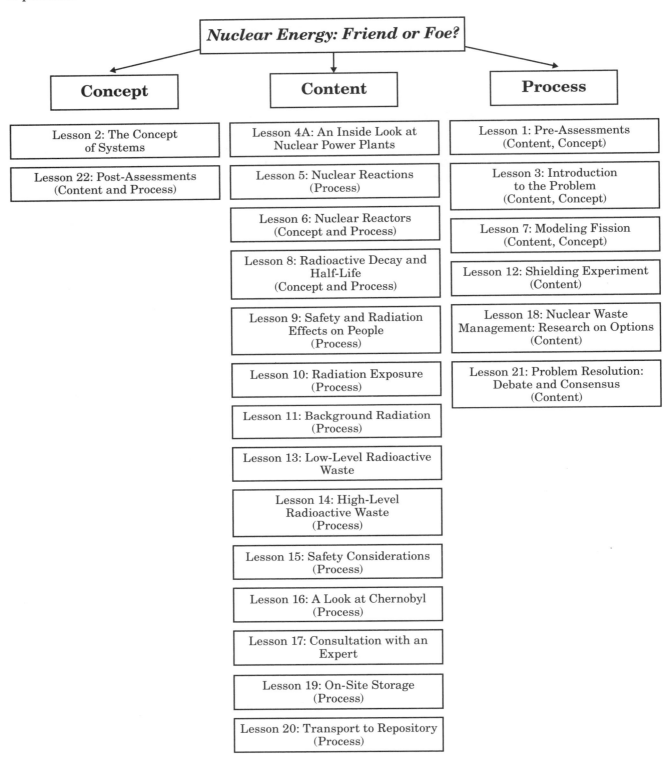

Nuclear Energy: Friend or Foe?

Concept	Content	Process
Lesson 2: The Concept of Systems	Lesson 4A: An Inside Look at Nuclear Power Plants	Lesson 1: Pre-Assessments (Content, Concept)
Lesson 22: Post-Assessments (Content and Process)	Lesson 5: Nuclear Reactions (Process)	Lesson 3: Introduction to the Problem (Content, Concept)
	Lesson 6: Nuclear Reactors (Concept and Process)	Lesson 7: Modeling Fission (Content, Concept)
	Lesson 8: Radioactive Decay and Half-Life (Concept and Process)	Lesson 12: Shielding Experiment (Content)
	Lesson 9: Safety and Radiation Effects on People (Process)	Lesson 18: Nuclear Waste Management: Research on Options (Content)
	Lesson 10: Radiation Exposure (Process)	Lesson 21: Problem Resolution: Debate and Consensus (Content)
	Lesson 11: Background Radiation (Process)	
	Lesson 13: Low-Level Radioactive Waste	
	Lesson 14: High-Level Radioactive Waste (Process)	
	Lesson 15: Safety Considerations (Process)	
	Lesson 16: A Look at Chernobyl (Process)	
	Lesson 17: Consultation with an Expert	
	Lesson 19: On-Site Storage (Process)	
	Lesson 20: Transport to Repository (Process)	

Content Background Information: Atoms, Isotopes, Fission, Nuclear Energy

Prerequisites for Students

This unit assumes that students have a basic working knowledge of atomic structure, the Periodic Table of the Elements and how to use it, and how to read chemical equations. If your students have not yet covered these topics, it would be advisable to introduce them before beginning the unit.

What Are Atoms and Isotopes? What Is Fission?

What Are Atoms?

An atom is the basic component of matter; all matter is divided into over one hundred different chemical elements. It is the smallest particle of the element having all the chemical properties of the element. The center of each atom is a nucleus, which is surrounded by electrons. The nucleus has positively-charged particles (protons) and neutral particles (neutrons). The electrons are negatively-charged particles. There is one electron for each proton in the atom.

What Are Isotopes?

An isotope is an atom with a specified number of protons and neutrons. The number of protons determines the chemical properties, so all atoms of the same chemical element have the same number of protons (and electrons). For example, element #92 is uranium, which has 92 protons in its nucleus.

However, the number of neutrons can change without changing chemical properties. So, there may be several isotopes of each element, each with similar chemical properties, but with differing nuclear properties. For example, there are three isotopes of uranium that exist in nature: uranium-238, uranium-235, and uranium-234. Their chemical properties are the same, while their nuclear properties differ. Uranium-238 has 92 protons and 146 neutrons for a total of 238 particles in its nucleus. Similarly, uranium-235 has 92 protons and 143 neutrons for a total of 235 particles in its nucleus.

What Is Fission?

Some isotopes are unstable, especially those with at least 92 protons, which are uranium and those with more protons than uranium (*transuranic elements*). Such atoms also have a large number of neutrons. Under certain conditions—especially when hit with a neutron—these unstable isotopes split, or fission, into two or three "fission products" and great amounts of energy.

The total amount of mass of these products is slightly less than the mass of the original atom. The missing mass has been changed into energy. The amount of energy is given by Albert Einstein's famous equation, $E = mc^2$, which means the

Source: United States Department of Energy http://www.gnep.energy.gov/pdfs/factSheetPrimerFuels.pdf

amount of mass times the speed of light, times the speed of light again, tells us the amount of energy.

The neutrons produced from fission keep the fission reaction going by interacting with other atoms and causing some of them to fission. Some of the neutrons cause other atoms to fission. The fission products are waste.

In a nuclear power plant, the energy from fission is converted into heat, turning water into steam, which then drives a turbine generator to produce electricity. Uranium and the transuranic elements are the source of heat for most nuclear power plants, rather than oil, coal or natural gas.

What Are Reactors? What Are Thermal or Fast Reactors?

A nuclear power plant generates electricity using a "reactor," which is a device designed to use the fission process (splitting of atoms) to turn a small amount of mass into energy in a controlled way. Each fission produces energy, neutrons, and waste fission products.

The energy from the fission reaction is removed from the reactor by a coolant to produce steam to drive the turbines of the electric generators. Thus, in a nuclear power plant, fission of nuclear fuel plays the same role as the burning of coal, natural gas, or oil plays in fossil fuel power plants. The neutrons cause more fission reactions.

There are two types of reactors: thermal-spectrum and fast-spectrum, or simply "thermal" or "fast" for short. The difference has to do with the energy level of the neutrons. The Global Energy Partnership includes both.

What Are Thermal Reactors?

In a thermal reactor, the neutrons created by fission are slowed down, or moderated, before they cause more fission reactions. Thermal reactors typically use a special type of uranium, called "enriched," and certain isotopes of the transuranic elements, called "fissile."

Virtually all of the world's 441 operating nuclear power plants are thermal reactors. Most of these are Light Water Reactors (LWRs), which use water to cool the reactor and to moderate (slow-down) neutrons. The two LWR types, boiling water reactors (BWRs) and pressurized water reactors (PWRs), result from early U.S. reactor development programs. LWRs dominate world nuclear energy because their technology is well proven and they have favorable economics compared to other options currently available.

What Are Fast Reactors?

In a fast reactor, the neutrons produced by fission are not slowed down (moderated) significantly before they cause more fission reactions. Thus, fast reactors must minimize use of materials, such as water, which slow neutrons. The higher energy neutrons can fission all types of uranium and transuranic elements, rather than only the "fissile" isotopes split in thermal reactors. This allows the fast reactor to transmute (consume) the transuranics efficiently and safely. Thus, fast reactors can extract energy from all types of uranium and all isotopes of the transuranic elements. The Global Nuclear Energy Partnership includes a type of fast reactor, which is designed to maximize consumption of transuranic elements. "Burner" in this instance doesn't mean incineration or combustion. It means conversion of transuranics into shorter-lived isotopes.

What Is Nuclear Fuel? What Does Nuclear Fuel Look Like?

What Does Nuclear Fuel Look Like?

Nuclear fuel is a solid material like coal or wood. It is not a liquid or gas like oil or propane. For U.S. nuclear power plants, uranium oxide fuel is made into pellets. The pellets are stacked into long tubes, typically made of an alloy of zirconium metal, to form fuel rods.

The fuel rods are bundled together and structurally reinforced to form a fuel assembly. These assemblies are installed in a nuclear reactor. The size and form of a nuclear fuel assembly depends on the type of reactor in which it will be used. There are typically hundreds of fuel assemblies in a single nuclear power plant.

What Is the Composition of New Light Water Reactor Nuclear Fuel?

The amount of isotope uranium-235 compared to isotope uranium-238 determines how energetic nuclear fuel is. Natural uranium is not energetic enough to use as fuel in light water reactors; it cannot sustain fission reactions. Instead, such reactors need uranium with a higher fraction of uranium-235 than is found in nature. This higher fraction is called "enriched." Light water reactors use fuel that is three to five percent uranium-235, whereas natural uranium is only 0.72 percent uranium-235.

What Is the Composition of Used Light Water Reactor Nuclear Fuel?

Used fuel that comes out of a power plant is only partially consumed. It has three major components: uranium, transuranic elements, and fission products.

- About 94 percent is uranium. It has lower energy content than uranium in fresh fuel, because the fraction of uranium-235 has fallen too low.
- About 1 percent are transuranic elements, which are those elements, like plutonium, that are beyond uranium in the periodic table; they are high-energy byproducts of neutron absorption in uranium.
- Less than 5 percent are fission products that result from splitting uranium or transuranic elements.

The uranium and transuranic elements in used nuclear fuel still have a great deal of residual energy. However, the used fuel must be removed from the nuclear power plant because of buildup fission products that stop the self-sustaining fission reaction.

Nuclear Fusion

Nuclear fusion is the process that powers the Sun, and for several decades people have looked to it as the answer to energy problems on Earth. However, the technological problems are complex, and a fusion power plant has not yet been built. (In 2005 agreement was reached between China, the European Union (EU), Japan, South Korea, Russia, and the United States on the building of the world's first nuclear fusion power plant at Cadarache, in southern France. The International Thermonuclear Experimental Reactor (ITER), as it is to be known, is scheduled to be in operation by 2016.) Fundamentally, any useful fusion reactor needs to confine plasma at a high enough density for sufficient time to generate more energy than the energy which was put in to create and confine the plasma. This occurs when the product of the confinement time and the density of the plasma, known as the Lawson number, is 10^{14} or above.

Numerous schemes for magnetic confinement of plasma have been tried since 1950. Thermonuclear reactions have been observed but the Lawson number has rarely exceeded 10^{12}. The Tokamak device, originally suggested in the USSR by Igor Tamm and Andrei Sakharov, began to give encouraging results in the 1960s.

The confinement chamber of a Tokamak has the shape of a torus (doughnut), with a minor diameter of about 1 m (3 ft 4 in) and a major diameter of about 3 m (9 ft 9 in). A toroidal magnetic field of about 5 tesla is established inside this chamber by large electromagnets. This is about 100,000 times the Earth's magnetic field at the planet's surface. A longitudinal current of several million amperes is induced in the plasma by the transformer coils that link the torus. The resulting magnetic field lines are spirals in the torus, and confine the plasma.

Following the successful operation of small Tokamaks at several laboratories, two large devices were built in the early 1980s, one at Princeton University in the United States and one in the USSR. In the Tokamak, high plasma temperature naturally results from resistive heating by the very large toroidal current, and additional heating by neutral beam injection in the new large machines should result in ignition conditions.

Another possible route to fusion energy is that of inertial confinement. In this technique, the fuel (tritium or deuterium) is contained within a tiny pellet that is bombarded on several sides by a pulsed laser beam. This causes an implosion of the pellet, setting off a thermonuclear reaction that ignites the fuel. Several laboratories in the United States and elsewhere are currently pursuing this possibility.

A significant milestone was achieved in 1991 when the Joint European Torus (JET) in the United Kingdom produced for the first time a significant amount of power (about 1.7 million watts) from controlled nuclear fusion. And in 1993 researchers at Princeton University in the United States used the Tokamak Fusion Test Reactor (TFTR) to produce 5.6 million watts. However, both JET and TFTR consumed more energy than they produced in these tests.

There has been promising progress in fusion research around the world for several decades; however, it will take decades more to develop a practical fusion power plant. It has been estimated that an investment of $50–100 billion is needed to achieve this, but each year only $1.5 billion is being spent worldwide. The main areas where work is needed include: superconducting magnets; vacuum systems; cryogenic systems; plasma purity, heating, and diagnostic systems; sustainment of plasma current; and safety issues.

The JET project has achieved "breakeven" operation, where the fusion power generated exceeds the input power, but only by injecting tritium that has made the structure radioactive. ITER is scheduled to begin by 2016. A demonstration fusion power plant would be built about 15 years later and, if successful, commercial fusion power plants could be operating by about 2050. This timescale could be significantly delayed or accelerated by the rate of progress in understanding plasma behavior and by the rate of funding.

If fusion energy does become practicable it would offer the following advantages: (1) an effectively limitless source of fuel—deuterium from the ocean; (2) inherent safety, since the fusion reaction would not "run away" and the amount of radioactive material present is low; and (3) waste products that are less radioactive and simpler to handle than those from fission systems. However, the structure will become radioactive due to absorption of neutrons, so decommissioning will be a serious undertaking.

Alpha particle The positively charged particle emitted in the radioactive decay of certain radioactive atoms. An alpha particle is identical to the nucleus of the helium atom.

Assumption A conclusion based on one's own beliefs and presuppositions

Atom The smallest part of a chemical element that has all the chemical properties of that element

Atomic Number The number of protons in the nucleus of an atom. There is a separate atomic number for each element. The atomic number is used to identify atoms as gold, oxygen, or some other element.

Atomic Weight The sum of the protons and neutrons in the nucleus of an atom

Background Radiation The natural radioactivity in the environment. Background radiation consists of cosmic radiation from outer space, radiation from the radioactive elements in rocks and soil, and radiation from radon and its decay products in the air we breathe.

Beta Particle It is smaller than an alpha particle. A beta particle can pass through paper but may be stopped by glass such as that found in windows

Boundary of a System Something that indicates or fixes a limit on the extent of the system

Conductor Material that permits electrons to flow freely

Constant The factor or factors in an experiment that are kept the same and not allowed to vary

Control The part of an experiment that serves as a standard of comparison. A control is used to detect the effects of factors that should be kept constant but that vary.

Control Rod Rods that slide up and down in between the fuel assemblies in order to control the speed of the nuclear reaction; these rods contain cadmium and boron, two elements that absorb neutrons but do not fission. These rods act as sponges to absorb neutrons that might hit other uranium atoms and cause them to split.

Current Flow of charge; measured in units called amperes

Decay Product The isotope produced by the decay of a radioactive isotope

Dependent Variable The factor or variable that may change as a result of changes purposely made in the independent variable

Electromagnetic Spectrum The complete range of frequencies of electromagnetic waves from the lowest to the highest, including radio, infrared, visible light, ultraviolet X-ray, and gamma ray waves

Electron A subatomic particle with a negative charge. The electron circles the nucleus of an atom.

Element of a System A distinct part of the system; a component of a complex system (a subsystem)

Fission Splitting apart atoms with the result that large amounts of energy and one or more neutrons are released. The splitting of a nucleus into two lighter nuclei, accompanied by the emission of two or more neutrons and a significant amount of energy. Fission in a nuclear reactor is initiated by the nucleus absorbing a neutron. Nuclear power plants split the nuclei of uranium atoms.

Fuel Assembly Bound fuel rods containing uranium pellets that generate heat; a fuel assembly usually consists of approximately 240 fuel rods that are about 20 feet long and contain 200 fuel pellets. The nuclear reactor core is made up of a collection of fuel assemblies.

Gamma Rays Waves of electromagnetic energy that are very penetrating and are best shielded by lead; they are emitted during the decay of certain radioactive materials

Half-Life The rate of decrease of a radioactive element; the amount of time it takes for half of the atoms in a quantity of a radioisotope to decay

High-Level Radioactive Waste Radioactive materials at the end of a useful life cycle that must be properly disposed of, including: the highly radioactive material resulting from the reprocessing of spent nuclear fuel; irradiated reactor fuel; and other highly radioactive material that requires permanent isolation. High-level waste (HLW) is primarily in the form of spent fuel discharged from commercial nuclear power reactors.

Hypothesis A tentative explanation for an observation, phenomenon, or scientific problem that can be tested by further investigation

Implication A suggestion of likely or logical consequence; a logical relationship between two linked propositions or statements

Independent Variable The variable that is changed on purpose by the experimenter

Inference Act of reasoning from factual knowledge or evidence; interpretation based on observation

Input to a System Something that is put in the system; an addition to the components of the system

Isotope One or more atoms having the same atomic number but a different atomic mass number; atoms of the same element that have equal numbers of protons but differing numbers of neutrons

Low-Level Radioactive Waste A general term for a wide range of wastes having low levels of radioactivity. Industries; hospitals and medical, educational, or research institutions; private or government laboratories; and nuclear fuel cycle facilities (e.g., nuclear power reactors and fuel fabrication plants) that use radioactive materials generate low-level wastes as part of their normal operations. Low-level radioactive wastes containing source, special nuclear, or by-product material are acceptable for disposal in a land disposal facility. (Definition from http://www .nrc.gov/reading-rm/basic-ref/glossary/low-level-waste.html)

Monitored Retrievable Storage (MRS) Facility A temporary surface storage system being studied by the U.S. Department of Energy as part of an integrated system for disposing of spent nuclear fuel

Neutron A subatomic particle that appears in the nucleus of all atoms except hydrogen. Neutrons have no electrical charge.

Nuclear Chain Reaction In a nuclear chain reaction, a fissionable nucleus absorbs a neutron and splits into two smaller, nearly equal nuclei, releasing additional neutrons. These in turn can be absorbed by other fissionable nuclei, releasing still more neutrons. This gives rise to a self-sustaining reaction.

Nuclear Radiation Ionizing radiation (alpha, beta, and gamma) originating in the nuclei of radioactive atoms

Nuclear Waste Radioactive by-products from any activity, including energy production, weapons production, and medical treatment and research

Nucleus The central part of an atom that contains the protons and neutrons

Output from a System Something that is produced by the system; a product of the system interactions

Perspective An attitude, opinion, or position from which a person understands a situation or issue

Pressure Vessel The large container that surrounds and protects the reactor core; a pressure vessel's walls can be as thick as 9 inches and it can weigh up to 300 tons

Proton A subatomic particle in the nucleus of an atom with about the same mass as the neutron but carrying a positive charge

Radiation Energy emitted in the form of rays or particles that are potentially harmful to humans; it moves through space in the form of particles or electromagnetic waves

Radioactive A property of some materials whereby spontaneous emissions of alpha or beta particles or gamma rays occur; these particles and rays are potentially harmful to humans.

Radioactive Decay The process by which radioactive materials become less radioactive over time

Radioactivity The property possessed by some elements, such as uranium, of spontaneously emitting alpha or beta particles or gamma rays

Radioisotope A radioactive isotope of a chemical element. Radioisotopes may occur naturally, or they may be artificially created from normal isotopes of an element.

Reactor A large machine that heats water

Spent Fuel Fuel that is removed from a reactor; it is highly radioactive and produces a high level of heat

System A group of interacting, interrelated, or interdependent elements forming a complex whole

Transuranic Having an atomic number greater than 92; elements with atomic numbers higher than the atomic number for uranium (92)

Ultraviolet Light Light with wavelength shorter than visible light but longer than X-rays

Uranium A radioactive, toxic element of which U-238 is the most abundant in nature. It is mined and processed for use in research, nuclear fuels, and nuclear weapons.

Water Coolant Usually purified water, the coolant keeps the temperature at a low enough level that it will not damage the core

Nuclear Energy Materials List

Lessons	Items Needed
6	Aluminum baking pans
17	Audiovisual equipment for guest speaker
6	Boxes of birthday candles (For each group: 25 for the first trial, up to 15 for the second trial)
8	Brass paper fasteners (200 or more per group)
11	Block of dry ice, large enough to hold a peanut butter jar
2, 3, 4, 13, 14, 17	Chart paper
7	Cooking oil
11	Corrugated cardboard
7	Cream cheese or dip spreader (or similar dull knife)
11	Dark-colored fabric
5	Dominoes (100 or more)
6	Envelopes
8	Graph paper (3 sheets per student)
7	Grease pencil
6	Goggles
6	Kitchen matches, long
14	Maps of the United States, blank
2, 3, 4, 17	Markers
14	Markers, black thin line
6	Modeling clay
13	Paper (plain white copy paper)
7	Paper towels
11	Peanut butter jar
8	Pennies (200 or more per group)
5	Periodic Table of the Elements
11	Plastic tray to hold dry ice
12	Plastic UV protective glasses
12	Prism
11	Projector (movie or slide projector), to provide a beam of light
13	Resource materials about low-level radioactive waste
11	Resource materials about radiation
7, 11	Rubbing alcohol
6	Ruler

continued

Lessons	Items Needed
12	Shielding materials: cinderblocks, glass, plastic, aluminum, foil (anything that can be tested for its ability to block UV or visible light)
8	Shoe boxes
8	Six-sided dice (200 or more per group)
5, 6	Stopwatch
5	Table (large) or floor space
7	Teaspoon
12	Ultraviolet light detector (e.g., white cotton T-shirt washed in a detergent that contains brightening agents—All or Tide)
12	Ultraviolet light source (e.g., black lightbulb, plant grow lightbulb, or tensor desk lamp bulb)
7	Water
7	Water glass (small); should be marked with a grease pencil on the outside at the two-thirds-full level

Handout Explanation*

The handouts listed below are used throughout the unit to help structure and guide students' thinking about experimental design. A brief purpose statement is provided here about each handout.

Teachers can choose to post copies of these handouts around the classroom for students to reference while designing experiments instead of providing new copies in every experiment lesson.

Experimental Design Planner: *Forces students to think about the nuts and bolts of a good experiment; the intellectual details of the experiment*

Experimental Design Planner Checklist: *Provides students with standards for their experimental design and with the structure for revising it*

Experimental Protocol: *Provides students with a structure for the process of explicating the planned materials, methods, and data to be collected*

Laboratory Report: *Provides students with a list of important questions regarding the experiment they conducted and the results*

Problem Log: *The student's **Problem Log** is a written compilation of the student's thoughts about the problem. Most lessons contain suggested questions or a handout with questions for students to answer in their **Problem Logs.** The **Problem Log** should also be used by the student to record and store data and new information that he or she has obtained during the course of the unit. (For the **Problem Log,** each student should use either a three-ring binder or a composition book.)*

Student Brainstorming Guide: *Asks students questions designed to guide their thinking about possible experiments to answer the problem*

Tailoring <u>Nuclear Energy: Friend or Foe?</u> to Your Location

Classroom experience demonstrates that this unit is much more powerful when tailored for the location in which it is being presented. Accordingly, consider the following suggestions:

1. Involve local experts (nuclear engineers, nuclear power plant employees, town managers, local politicians, etc.) as speakers and ongoing resources in the problem-solving process. In addition to these experts, you may have a citizen's group that monitors issues dealing with the local nuclear power plant; a participant from such a group would also be a good resource.

*Note: These handouts are provided in the optional student book.

2. Work with media specialists to plan the unit and to assist students in finding resources. Other sources of support include special libraries (museums, corporations, historical societies, etc.); their staffs can offer information about resources relevant to the unit.

3. Identify your closest nuclear power plant and obtain information about it to develop a class display or project webpage.

4. Look for similar situations cited in the newspaper and use them as resources or points of comparison.

Laboratory Safety Precautions

As this unit involves laboratory work, some general safety procedures must be observed at all times. Most school districts have prescribed laboratory safety rules; for those that do not, some basic rules to follow for scientific experimentation are:

1. Appropriate behavior in the lab includes no running or horseplay; materials should be used for intended purposes only.
2. Eating or drinking is prohibited in the lab; there should be no tasting of laboratory materials.
3. If students are using heat sources, such as alcohol burners, long hair must be tied back and loose clothing should be covered by a lab coat. Long sleeves should be rolled or pushed up on the arms.
4. Fire extinguishers must be available; students should know where they are and how to use them.

Specific safety rules relevant to implementing this unit are:

1. Students should wear goggles when working with candles and matches.
2. The room or laboratory should be well ventilated, as certain experiments may produce a great deal of smoke.
3. Cream cheese or dip spreaders have been substituted for butter knives in this unit. Students should be cognizant of the potential danger in using these untensils.
4. Radioactive materials are hazardous. Please follow all safety guidelines provided by the supplier of the materials.

_____   _____
Student Signature   Date

_____   _____
Teacher Signature   Date

Dear Family,

Your child is about to begin a unique science experience that utilizes an instructional strategy called problem-based learning. In this unit, students will take an active role in identifying and resolving a real-world problem constructed to promote scientific learning. Your child will be gathering information from a variety of sources both in and out of school in order to contribute to the problem resolution. Goals for the unit are:

Goal 1 To understand the concept of systems.

Goal 2 To understand the principles of fusion and fission and the effect of their products on humans and the environment.

Goal 3 To understand and apply the basic principles of experimental design.

Goal 4 To develop reasoning skills with application to science.

Good curriculum and instructional practice should involve parents as well as teachers. We know from educational research that parental involvement is a strong factor in promoting positive attitudes toward science, and we encourage you to extend your child's school learning through activities in the home.

Ways you may wish to help your child during this unit include the following:

- Discussing systems, including family systems, educational systems, and so on with your child.

- Allowing your child to describe the problem and the day's outcomes to you, and trying to solve the problem along with your child.

- Engaging your child in scientific experimentation exercises based on everyday events. For example, in a grocery store, how would you test whether it is better to go in a long line with people who have few items or a short line with people who have full carts?

- Visiting area science museums and the library to explore how scientists solve problems.

- Using the problem-based learning model to question students about an issue they might have about the real world. For example, how does hail form? Answer: What do you know about hail? What do you need to know to answer the question? How do you find out?

Thank you in advance for your interest in your child's curriculum. Please do not hesitate to contact me for additional information as the unit progresses.

Sincerely,

2

Lesson Plans

Pre-Assessments

Instructional Purpose

- To assess student understanding of nuclear energy
- To assess student understanding of experimental design
- To assess student understanding of systems

Curriculum Alignment  **Goal 1** Concept  **Goal 2** Content  **Goal 3** Process/ Experimental Design ○ **Goal 4** Process/ Reasoning

---

 Materials/Resources

- Content Pre-Assessment (Handout 1.1)
- Content Pre-Assessment Scoring Guide (Teacher Resource 1)
- Experimental Design Pre-Assessment (Handout 1.2)
- Experimental Design Rubric (Teacher Resource 2)
- Systems Pre-Assessment (Handout 1.3)
- Systems Pre-Assessment Scoring Guide (Teacher Resource 3)
- Problem Logs

Lesson Length

Three 20-minute sessions

 **Activities**

1. Explain to students that they will be beginning a new unit of study focused on scientific inquiry. Tell students that in order to get a good sense of how much they already know and to be able to tell how much they have learned by the end of the unit, they will need to take several pre-assessments. Distribute the **Pre-Assessments** (Handouts 1.1, 1.2, and 1.3) and have students complete them individually. You may wish to have the students complete the pre-assessments in three 20-minute sessions.

2. Collect and score the **Pre-Assessments.** The

Pre-Assessments may be evaluated using the **Scoring Guides** (Teacher Resources 1, 2, and 3).

3. Have students discuss which aspects of the **Pre-Assessments** they found difficult. Explain that throughout the unit they will be thinking about challenging questions that relate to concepts on the **Pre-Assessments.**

 ## Problem Log

Have students respond to one of the following prompts:

- I want to learn more about these things in science . . .
- Studying science can help me in the following ways . . .
- It is important to know about science because . . .
- It is important to know about nuclear energy because . . .
- Knowing about nuclear energy will enable me to . . .

 ## Notes

1. Send home the parent letter with each student who will be participating in the unit.

2. The **Pre-Assessments** given in this lesson serve multiple purposes. Performance on the **Pre-Assessments** should establish a baseline against which performance on the **Post-Assessments** may be compared. In addition, teachers may use information obtained from **Pre-Assessments** to aid instructional planning, as strengths and areas for improvement among students become apparent.

3. Students should have a unit notebook and folder that they can use throughout the unit to respond to **Problem Log Questions** and other written assignments and to keep any handouts from the unit. The notebook can also hold a running list of unit vocabulary, which also can be displayed in the classroom in chart form.

 ## Homework

- Have students make a list describing attributes of scientists. Encourage them to generate as many different ideas as they can.

 ## Assessment

- **Pre-Assessments**
- **Problem Log**

 ## Technology Integration

- If the resources are available, students may keep their Problem Logs in electronic format rather than in paper-and-pencil format.

Name _____   Date _____

Content Pre-Assessment

In the space provided, record what you know about the risks of nuclear energy and about its potential as a resource.

Nuclear Energy	
Risks	Potential as a resource

Content Pre-Assessment Scoring Guide
(Teacher Resource 1)

In the space provided, record what you know about the risks of nuclear energy and about its potential as a resource.

Nuclear Energy	
Risks	Potential as a resource
– *Risk of accidents* – *Risk of diversion of materials for harmful uses* – *Nuclear waste storage* – *Nuclear waste disposal* – *Other reasonable responses*	– *Provides an alternative to other energy sources* – *Nuclear waste can be recycled to produce more energy* – *Other reasonable responses*

Experimental Design Pre-Assessment

Among the furniture, clothing, jewelry, books, dolls, dishes, and many other objects sold at flea markets and antique shops, you will likely find items that contain radioactive compounds. These items were generally made and originally sold before the health effects of radiation were well understood and long before radiation protection regulations were put into place. Certain items such as clocks, watches, and instrument dials that glow in the dark contain radium or tritium. Old ceramics get their color from the addition of various radionuclides to their glaze. These items emit small amounts of radiation but enough to register on a handheld Geiger counter.

Construct a fair test of the following question: *How can I dispose of my collection of old watches and be sure there are no lasting emissions of radiation?*

Describe in detail how you would test this question. Be as scientific as you can as you write about your test. Write the steps you would take to find out how to dispose of the collection of watches, ensuring that there will be no lasting radiation emissions.

Adapted from Fowler, M. (1990). The diet cola test. *Science Scope, 13(4)*, 32–34.

Teacher Resource 2: Experimental Design Rubric

Criteria	Strong Evidence 2	Some Evidence 1	No Evidence 0	Pre	Post
States **PROBLEM** or **QUESTION.**	Clearly states the problem or question to be addressed.	Somewhat states the problem or question to be addressed.	Does not state the problem or question to be addressed.		
Generates a **PREDICTION** and/or **HYPOTHESIS.**	Clearly generates a prediction or hypothesis appropriate to the experiment.	Somewhat generates a prediction or hypothesis appropriate to the experiment.	Does not generate a prediction or hypothesis.		
Lists experiment steps.	Clearly & concisely lists four or more steps as appropriate for the experiment design.	Clearly & concisely lists one to three steps as appropriate for the experiment design.	Does not generate experiment steps.		
Arranges steps in **SEQUENTIAL** order.	Lists experiment steps in sequential order.	Generally lists experiment steps in sequential order.	Does not list experiment steps in a logical order.		
Lists **MATERIALS** needed.	Provides an inclusive and appropriate list of materials.	Provides a partial list of materials needed.	Does not provide a list of materials needed.		
Plans to **REPEAT TESTING** and tells reason.	Clearly states a plan to conduct multiple trials, providing reasoning.	Clearly states a plan to conduct multiple trials.	Does not state plan or reason to repeat testing.		
DEFINES the terms of the experiment.	Correctly defines all relevant terms of the experiment.	Correctly defines some of the relevant terms of the experiment.	Does not define terms, or defines terms incorrectly.		
Plans to **MEASURE.**	Clearly identifies plan to measure data.	Provides some evidence of planning to measure data.	Does not identify plan to measure data.		
Plans **DATA COLLECTION.**	Clearly states plan for data collection, including note-taking, the creation of graphs or tables, etc.	States a partial plan for data collection.	Does not identify a plan for data collection.		
States plan for **INTERPRETING DATA.**	Clearly states plan for interpreting data by comparing data, looking for patterns and reviewing previously known information.	States a partial plan for interpreting data.	Does not state plan for interpreting data.		
States plan for drawing a **CONCLUSION BASED ON DATA.**	Clearly states plan for drawing conclusions based on data.	States a partial plan for drawing conclusions based on data.	Does not state plan for drawing conclusions.		

TOTAL SCORE:

Adapted from Fowler, M. (1990). The diet cola test. *Science Scope, 13(4)*, 32–34.

Name _____   Date _____

Systems Pre-Assessment

Think of how a swimming pool is an example of a system.

1. List the parts of the system in the spaces that follow. Include boundaries, elements, input, and output.

   Boundaries:

   Elements:

   Inputs:

   Outputs:

2. Draw a diagram of the system showing where each of the parts is located.

Systems Pre-Assessment Scoring Guide
(Teacher Resource 3)

Think of how a swimming pool is an example of a system.

1. **(25 points)** List the parts of the system. Include boundaries, elements, inputs, and outputs.

   Boundaries: (10 points)

   The boundaries of this system are the walls and surface of the pool (including the drain but not the sewer).

   Note: *Students may have different boundaries for this system. As long as their other answers in this section are consistent with these boundaries, accept their answers.*

   Give ten points for clearly specified boundaries. These boundaries should completely enclose the system; there should be no question about whether something is inside the system or not. If the boundaries described are only partially complete, give only five points; if no boundaries are described at all, give zero points.

   Elements: (5 points)

   The elements of the system are the pool water, algal spores, bacteria, the surface of the pool walls, the drain and filter basket, etc.

   Give two points for a single reasonable item; give five points for any answer that has two or more reasonable items.

   Inputs: (5 points)

   The inputs of the system are the fresh tap water, rainwater, students and their by-products, bacteria, viruses, suntan oil, dirt, rocks, pool toys, bugs, leaves, pool chemicals, sunlight, frogs, etc.

   Give two points for a single reasonable item; give five points for any answer that has two or more reasonable items.

   Outputs: (5 points)

   The outputs of the system are the pool water that splashes out of the pool, water that evaporates, oxygen made by the algae, dirty water that leaves the pool through the drains, water that leaves on the surfaces of students, etc.

Give two points for a single reasonable item; give five points for any answer that has two or more reasonable items.

2. **(10 points)** Draw a diagram of the system that shows where each of the parts can be found.

Give ten points for a drawing that includes all of the system components listed by the student in his or her answer to part one; give five points for a drawing that includes only some of the system components listed in the student's answer to part one.

Total number of points possible: 35

The Concept of Systems

2

Instructional Purpose

• To introduce the concept of systems

Curriculum Alignment

 Goal 1 — Concept   ○ Goal 2 — Content   ○ Goal 3 — Process/Experimental Design   ○ Goal 4 — Process/Reasoning

 ## Vocabulary

Boundary Something that includes a border or limit

Dysfunctional Not working properly

Element A fundamental or essential part of something

Input Something put into a system or used in its operation to achieve an output or a result

Interaction Mutual action or influence of one element, individual, or group with another; a process occurring among elements of a system

Interdependent Mutually relying on or requiring the aid of another

Output A product of a system; a product of the system interactions

Productive Effective in achieving specified results

System A group of interactive, interrelated, or interdependent elements that form a complex whole

 ## Materials/Resources

• Chart paper
• Markers
• Systems Diagram (Handout 2.1)
• Systems Model (Handout 2.2)
• System Parts Chart (Handout 2.3)
• Problem Logs

Lesson Length

120 minutes

 ## Activities

1. Explain to the students that the concept of **systems** will be the basis of their scientific inquiry throughout this unit. Divide students into small groups. Instruct each group to draw the outline of a refrigerator. Explain that a refrigerator is an example of a system. Ask

35

students to illustrate and label the refrigerator and discuss what things it contains and what is put into and comes out of it regularly. Discuss the refrigerator as a class and tell students that they can define five things about systems: **elements, boundaries, inputs, outputs,** and **interactions.** Record the terms on chart paper and have students record them in their **Problem Logs.**

2. Use the following questions to help students understand each of these terms:

    Elements What are the parts of the refrigerator? What is inside the refrigerator? What else has to be a part of the refrigerator so that it does its job?

    Boundaries What keeps the elements of the refrigerator together? What are the edges of the system?

    Inputs What things go into the refrigerator from the outside? What are some things that have to be part of this system on a regular basis in order to keep the food from spoiling?

    Outputs What things come out of the refrigerator?

    Interactions What are some of the things that happen in the refrigerator to use the inputs and produce the outputs? How does the refrigerator use the inputs and give off outputs?

3. Tell students that there are many different kinds of systems. Some systems are small and their boundaries, elements, inputs, and outputs are easy to identify while other systems are more complex. Some systems contain living things while others do not. Distribute the **Systems Diagram** (Handout 2.1) and have students complete the diagram using the classroom system as an example. Discuss the elements, boundaries, inputs, outputs, and interactions of the classroom system.

4. Have students return to their small groups. Give each group a sheet of chart paper and markers. Ask groups to brainstorm additional systems given their new understanding of a system's characteristics. Use questions such as the following to help start students' thinking:

    • What are some examples of systems?

    • What are some systems in nature?

    • What are some systems that are man-made?

    • What makes these things systems?

    • Can you identify their elements, boundaries, inputs, outputs, and interaction?

    • How do you decide if something is a system?

5. Encourage each group to share its examples and reasoning with the class. Make a class list of systems. Ask students to work in their groups in order to put the systems into categories. Use the following questions to help students categorize their systems:

    • How could you separate these systems into different groups?

    • What are some things that a few of the systems might have in common?

- Once you have put your systems into groups, what would you call each group?
- How did you decide which group of systems went together?
- Do all of your systems fall into groups?
- Do some of your systems fit into more than one group? Which ones?

6. Next, tell students that in order to understand what a system is, it helps to understand what a system is not. Give an example from the refrigerator. Explain that a shelf in the refrigerator is an element of the refrigerator system but that it is not a system by itself. Explain that although a shelf's elements and boundaries can be defined, it does not function as a system because there are no interactions *within* the shelf itself. Have students brainstorm a list of things that are not systems. Discuss each of the student suggestions and determine why they are or are not systems.

7. Ask students if they can give any generalizations or true statements about systems in general. Distribute the **Systems Model** (Handout 2.2) and introduce the concept generalizations. Explain to students that these generalizations will serve as a framework for their entire unit of study. Use the following questions to help students complete the model using the school as the system. Have students record the generalizations in their **Problem Logs.**

   - *The interactions and outputs of a system change when its inputs, elements, or boundaries change.* What interactions in the school system would be different if all students wore uniforms? What output changes would occur if there were not enough classrooms for every student in the school?

   - *Systems can be productive or dysfunctional.* What are examples of when the school is productive or dysfunctional? How do you know? What causes the school system to be productive or dysfunctional?

   - *Many systems are made up of smaller systems.* How does the discipline system affect the school system? What other smaller systems exist within the school?

   - *Systems are interdependent.* How are the smaller systems within the school related? What would happen without one of them? What other systems would enhance our school system?

   - *All systems have patterns.* Ask students to identify patterns in their school system, such as the bells ringing at scheduled times that are repeated each day or each week.

8. Discuss a city as an example of a system. Ask questions such as:
   - Is there a boundary to the city? What is it?
   - What are some of the elements in the city? Can these elements be categorized?
   - What would be the input into the city?
   - What is the output from the city?
   - What are some of the ways the city elements interact with each other?

9. Have students complete the **System Parts Chart** (Handout 2.3).

 **Notes**

1. This lesson may take more than one class period to complete. Stages of the model can be expanded as necessary to ensure student understanding and may be completed in small groups or as a whole class. Lessons throughout the unit will refer to the list of generalizations included in this lesson. These generalizations should be posted in the classroom and students should keep their **Systems Diagram** and **Systems Model** in their **Problem Logs** for reference throughout the unit. The concept development model employed in this lesson is explained in detail in the implementation guidelines at the end of the unit.

2. Using the classroom as a system may be meaningful to the children because they have prior knowledge of this system; however, select any system that students are familiar with as an example.

 Homework

- Have students complete the **Systems Model** with examples of how the system generalizations apply to a system in their home. It may be helpful for them to refer to the completed **Systems Diagram.**

 Extending Student Learning

- Have students build a model or draw a diagram of a nuclear power plant, marking inputs, outputs, and other parts of the system.

 Assessment

- Participation in class discussion
- Completed **Systems Model**
- Completed **System Parts Chart**
- **Problem Logs:** Students should have noted the elements, boundaries, inputs, outputs, and interactions in their home system. Clear connections to the generalizations and systems vocabulary should be present.

Name _____ Date _____

Systems Diagram

Name of System _____

Boundaries

Elements

Inputs

Outputs

Interactions

Name _____   Date _____

Systems Model

Name of System _____

Give examples of how the system demonstrates each generalization.

The interactions and outputs of a system change when its inputs, elements, or boundaries change.
Systems can be productive or dysfunctional.
Many systems are made up of smaller systems.
Systems are interdependent.
All systems have patterns.

System Parts Chart

1. What are the boundaries of the system? Why did you choose them? Were there other possibilities?

2. List some important elements of the system.

3. Describe inputs into the system. Where do they come from?

4. Describe outputs from the system. What part(s) of the system produce them?

continued

5. Describe some important interactions

   a. among system elements.

   b. between system elements and inputs into the system.

6. What would happen to the system if the interactions in 5a could not take place? In 5b?

Introduction to the Problem

3

Instructional Purpose
- To introduce students to the initial problem statement
- To begin using problem-based learning

Curriculum Alignment

 **Goal 1** Concept   **Goal 2** Content  **Goal 3** Process/ Experimental Design  **Goal 4** Process/ Reasoning

 Vocabulary

Assumption Conclusions based on one's own beliefs and presuppositions

Fission Splitting apart atoms with the result that large amounts of energy and one or more neutrons are released. The splitting of a nucleus into two lighter nuclei, accompanied by the emission of two or more neutrons and a significant amount of energy. Fission in a nuclear reactor is initiated by the nucleus absorbing a neutron. Nuclear power plants split the nuclei of uranium atoms.

Implication A suggestion of likely or logical consequence; a logical relationship between two linked propositions or statements

Perspective An attitude, opinion, or position from which a person understands a situation or issue

Stakeholder A person who has an interest in or involvement with an enterprise or issue and its potential outcomes

Uranium A radioactive, toxic element of which U-238 is the most abundant in nature. It is mined and processed for use in research, nuclear fuels, and nuclear weapons.

Materials/Resources

- Initial Problem Statement (Handout 3.1)
- Need to Know Board (Handout 3.2)
- Problem Log Questions (Handout 3.3)
- Problem Log Questions (Handout 3.4)
- Problem Log Questions (Handout 3.5)

- Need to Know Board on chalkboard or chart paper
- Nuclear Energy and Nuclear Waste Supplementary Information for Lesson 3
- Additional Information About Riverton (Handout 3.6)
- Riverton Map (Handout 3.7)
- CAFSE Letter to Residents (Handout 3.8)
- Background Notes: Acme Power's Maple Island Nuclear Power Facility (Handout 3.9)
- Cancer Patients in Riverton (1994-1995) (Handout 3.10)
- Acme Power Memorandum: Office of the Director (Handout 3.11)
- Newspaper Article, "Silent Holocaust" (Handout 3.12)
- CAFSE Newspaper Article (Handout 3.13)
- Acme Power Memorandum: Department of Waste Management (Handout 3.14)
- City of Riverton Ordinance 829-85 and Amendment (Handout 3.15)
- Memo to the Mayor (Handout 3.16)

Lesson Length

Three 60-minute sessions

 ## Session 1 Activities

1. Ask students to write everything they know about systems in their **Problem Logs** without using resources. Review the concept generalizations and vocabulary as a class. Have students share their homework.

2. Distribute copies of the **Initial Problem Statement** (Handout 3.1) and read it together as a class. Explain to students that they will be taking the role of the mayor of the town, and they need to begin learning about nuclear energy in order to make informed decisions. Have students staple or glue the **Initial Problem Statement** into their **Problem Logs.**

3. Introduce the **Need to Know Board** (Handout 3.2) and explain that it is a tool to help organize important information about the problem as well as to record questions and resources. (In the first column, students list the information that they can glean from the **Initial Problem Statement;** they should list only information that is given in the problem statement. In the second column, students should list the types of additional information needed for working through the problem. In the third column, students should list ways they can find the needed information and also potential sources of the information.) Complete the chart as a class and record information on the chalkboard or chart paper. Ask students to clarify the importance of their ideas by asking for more information. Also encourage them to begin formulating their ideas about what the problem is.

4. Prioritize the **Need to Know Board** from "most" to "least critical." Debate reasons for prioritizing choices. Ask students to identify resources that will

help them answer or further investigate the elements of the **Need to Know Board.** Divide the learning issues among students so that each student (or a different group of students) will bring different information to the class during the following session.

5. Have students identify key words and phrases as they organize elements of the problem. Record new or key words and phrases on the chalkboard or chart paper. Students should devote a section of their **Problem Logs** to recording new or key words.

6. Ask students to identify resources that will help them answer or further investigate the issue. Allow small groups to choose which part of the issue they would like to investigate. Small groups should self-assign information to bring to the next class meeting.

7. Have students complete **Problem Log Questions** (Handout 3.3).

8. **Ask:**
   - What's happening?
   - What are we supposed to do?
   - What kinds of questions do you think the press will ask you?
   - What are the questions you have in your mind?
   - What additional information would you like to have about the power plant? About CAFSE's side of the issue?
   - Where can we find the answers to these questions?
   - Do you have any ideas right now about what to do?
   - What seems to be the main problem?
   - Are there other problems? What could they be?
   - What's the best way to proceed to get this information?

Session 2 Notes

1. Prior to this session, assemble the supplementary information pages (at the end of this lesson) into packets for various groups.

2. The supplementary information presented in this lesson was generated as a result of questions asked by the pilot test classes as they tried to unravel the problem. It is possible that other students will raise questions that are not answered by these documents. Teachers may have to supplement this information with their own original documents.

Session 2 Activities

1. Provide the additional information about the expansion issue (best if provided as "primary sources"—medical reports, letters, diagrams, maps, etc.). You may distribute the packets that contain the supplementary information found at the end of this lesson. Allow for some time for in-class research if necessary, or assign a "task force" to go to the library.

2. Have students report on the information they found overnight. Ask them to review the **Need to Know Board** and identify (a) what questions they have answered, and (b) what new questions arise out of their new information. Next, ask students what they are going to need to know in order to solve the problem. Prioritize the list based on negotiations with students.

3. Encourage students to refine their speculations about the nature of the problem, the size of the problem, and the pervasiveness of the problem. (Is this just a problem for Riverton or is it a problem for other people in the state? The country?)

4. **Ask:**

   • What questions are answered by the new information?

   • What questions do we still have to answer?

   • What new questions do you have?

   • What are the things we may have to learn about to address the problem?

   • Is the problem different today than it was yesterday?

   • How are we going to solve this problem?

   • What sort of strategies should we use?

5. Have students complete **Problem Log Questions** (Handout 3.4).

 Session 3 Activities

1. Discuss the upcoming Town Meeting and how to best present a full picture of nuclear energy to the public.

2. Students should refer to the public notice from the mayor and select specific phrases that would be important for the public to understand.

3. Through tutorial questioning and reference to the **Need to Know Board,** students can spend a full session developing a list of information about nuclear energy.

4. Specific topics can be assigned to individuals or groups of students to investigate. Give out **Problem Log Questions** (Handout 3.5) to help students focus on their areas of interest.

5. **Ask:**

   • What information does the public need to understand about nuclear energy in order to make an informed decision at the town meeting?

   • What scientific knowledge will we have to present at the meeting for the public to understand nuclear energy?

   • What group or groups do you think will be attending the Town Meeting?

   • What do you think their primary concerns will be?

   • What kinds of questions do you think these people will want to have answered?

   • In order to understand the main nuclear energy questions, what specific questions do we need to have answered?

- Are we outlining information that is unbiased?
- Will understanding this information help the public to see both the positive and negative issues of nuclear power?

Notes

1. The initial problem statement sets the stage for students to start asking questions about nuclear energy and systems. However, the **Additional Problem Statement Information** provides a sense of urgency as well as introducing the students to some of the problems that are faced by scientists and community members regarding nuclear energy.

2. Many activities in this unit require students to work in groups. Determine whether you will maintain the same groups throughout the unit or vary them depending on the tasks.

3. The student **Need to Know Boards** should be stapled or glued into their **Problem Logs.** They may be copied onto chart paper and posted around the room to be used as working documents throughout the unit.

4. The Research Model (see Implementation Guide) may be used throughout the unit to guide student research.

Homework

- Students are responsible for bringing information to class as agreed upon in Step 6 of Session 1. Information should be written down but does not have to be in paragraph form. Students should bring the sources of their information to class.

Extending Student Learning

- Have students complete a **Systems Diagram** for one of the systems mentioned in the problem statement.

Assessment

- Completed **Need to Know Board**
- Active and appropriate participation in group and class discussions
- **Problem Log Questions:** Students should utilize information from the class discussion to frame their answers.

Technology Integration

- Online research can be conducted about current events related to nuclear energy production and the problems that are encountered in the field.

Initial Problem Statement

Your name is Christine Barrett, and you are the mayor of the town of Riverton. You have a nice home on the Back River with your husband Richard, a middle-school teacher for the Riverton School District, and six-year-old son Ellis, now entering the first grade.

Your job as mayor has been rough at times, but you still enjoy it. The aspect of the town that has been giving you the most grief recently has been the Maple Island Nuclear Power Plant, the largest industry in Riverton. It produces power for not only Riverton but nearly half of the state also.

Yesterday, you received a letter from your long-time friend, Jerry Brown, Vice President of Waste Management for the Maple Island Nuclear Power Plant. He was writing regarding a suggested plan for expanding the waste disposal pools at the plant to accommodate the growing number of used power assemblies.

Today you receive a letter from CAFSE (Citizens Action for a Safe Environment) adamantly opposing not only the expansion of the power plant but also the fact that the plant is operating at all. An open discussion on the proposed expansion has already been slated for next month's town council meeting. You have only five weeks to garner support for whatever position you take.

Name _____   Date _____

Need to Know Board

What we know . . .	What we need to know . . .	How we can find out . . .

Problem Log Questions

As the problem evolves, keep a list of the issues you think are associated with the **Initial Problem Statement.** Use this list to help organize your thinking and record the connections between the pieces of information or ideas you are developing.

Problem Log Questions

1. After our initial discussions, what do you think the problem really is?

    - Why do you think this is the main problem?

    - Is it the same problem you thought was the main problem when we first began our discussion?

    - If not, how has the problem changed?

    - What are the issues you are most interested in researching?

continued

2. Look at this issue from another viewpoint.

- What will the similarities of the old and new perspectives be?

- What will the differences be?

Name _____   Date _____

Problem Log Questions

Now that we have created a comprehensive class list of the questions surrounding nuclear energy, create a detailed specific list of questions surrounding the particular topic you want to investigate.

Nuclear Energy and Nuclear Waste Supplementary Information for Lesson 3

Note to the Teacher

The majority of the materials presented in this section elaborate on the problem presented in the pilot testing of the unit. Included are the letters, newspaper articles, a map of Riverton, some general information, descriptions of the Barretts and the Maple Island Nuclear Power Plant, and incidence rates of cancer in Riverton.

If the information seems somewhat disjointed, it is because it was developed to answer specific questions raised by students during the pilot testing of the unit. Assuming that other students will think of similar questions, the materials were included. However, these materials may not answer all of the questions that another creative group of students could imagine. Teachers are encouraged to supplement the story with information of their own making; what is important is that the information presented remains factual and that the representation of the information be as "authentic" as possible.

Included as supplementary information are the following:

- Additional Information About Riverton
- Riverton Map
- CAFSE Letter to Residents
- Background Notes: Acme Power's Maple Island Nuclear Power Facility
- Cancer Patients in Riverton (1994–1995)
- Acme Power Memorandum: Office of the Director
- Newspaper Article, "Silent Holocaust"
- CAFSE Newspaper Article
- Acme Power Memorandum: Department of Waste Management
- City of Riverton Ordinance 829-85 and Amendment
- Memo to the Mayor

Additional Information About Riverton

Background Information: The Barretts and Maple Island

The Barretts have lived in Riverton, Virginia, since 1972. Their home is located 5.2 miles from the Maple Island Nuclear Power Plant—the facility that serves as an energy source for the area. In fact, 33 percent of the energy that supplies the community comes from this facility. The plant was built in 1970 and there have been no problems of which the public has been aware, until now. Acme Power Company owns the Maple Island Nuclear Power Plant. Up to this point, you have tried to balance the different sides of the power plant issue to try to appease as many parties as possible. You realize that whatever decision you make will inevitably upset one of the groups. You thought of "passing the buck" along to the state or U.S. government to make the decision, but the other day there was a message from Congressman Paul Greene, a representative to the U.S. Congress from the local Congressional District. Congressman Greene has received both letters of complaint from CAFSE and letters from power plant workers concerned about losing their jobs. He believes you could better solve this controversy than he could, since you know all the parties involved better than he does.

Riverton Map

1 inch = 4 miles

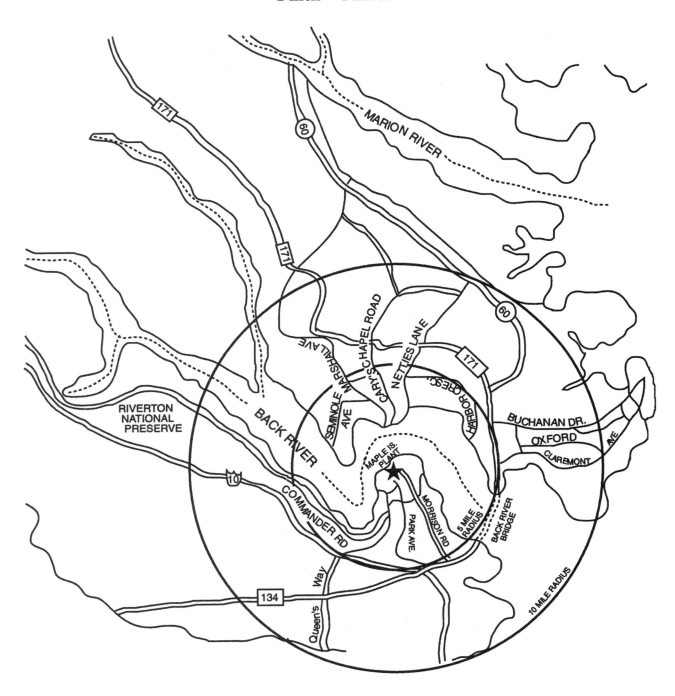

CAFSE Letter to Residents

Citizens for a Safe Environment
1234 Jamestown Road
Riverton, VA 08934-1882

Dear Resident,

Is our community safe? Towns across the nation are beginning to ask this question. As nuclear power plants proliferate, so do many potential dangers. Our water and our environment are endangered by these facilities, and our health may be too. Incidence of cancer is on the rise in Riverton, especially among our children. Members of Citizens for a Safe Environment (CAFSE) believe that the Maple Island Nuclear Power Facility owned by Acme Power is directly related to the increased frequency of the disease. We urge you to join our efforts to CLOSE THE PLANT and make Riverton safe for our children again.

For more information about CAFSE, call Rebecca Weaver at 555-555-1234.

Sincerely,

CAFSE Membership

Background Notes: Acme Power's Maple Island Nuclear Power Facility

The Maple Island Nuclear Generating Plant in Riverton, Virginia, has two Westinghouse pressurized water reactors, which produce nearly 33 percent of Acme Electric Power Company's electrical power. This nuclear facility originally had 210 fuel assemblies, which made up the reactor core; the plant is shut down for refueling approximately every 3 years. When this refueling occurs, approximately seventy fuel assemblies (one-third of the reactor core) are removed from the reactor and replaced with new fuel assemblies. The spent-fuel assemblies are then moved to the spent-fuel pools for storage.

"Spent fuel" consists of reactor fuel assemblies that have been irradiated in the reactor core until they have been exhausted, or "spent," as a fuel source. These assemblies contain highly radioactive fission products, which include uranium, plutonium, strontium-90, iodine, and cesium-137. Each of these by-products is potentially dangerous.

The spent-fuel assemblies at the Maple Island nuclear facility are no longer able to sustain normal reactor operation efficiently: thus, they must be removed from the reactor. Fissionable materials remain in the spent fuel, and they are capable of maintaining a nuclear reaction. For this reason, the Acme Power Company originally planned to send the spent fuel (following short-term on-site storage) to a nuclear fuel repository in order to permanently store it safely.

Two spent-fuel pools were built in order to provide the capacity to safely store 210 fuel assemblies. The smaller pool was intended primarily to handle a spent-fuel shipping cask; the larger of the two pools was designed to store spent nuclear fuel. The racks were constructed so that fuel assemblies are stored vertically, each in its own cavity. It is important that the assemblies be kept far enough apart in order to prevent a sustained nuclear reaction. Because water moderates the hot spent fuel and acts as a shield from radiation, all fuel-handling operations in the pool are performed under water.

In the early 1980s, it became apparent that the permanent repository proposed in the Nuclear Waste Policy Act of 1982 would not be fully operational in time to take spent fuel from the Maple Island Plant—so a modification project was initiated in 1985 to increase the pool storage capacity. The new pool layout, which used existing space more efficiently, expanded the capacity from 210 fuel assemblies to 687.

After the modification project, spent-fuel assemblies continued to accumulate in the pool. Acme claims that shutdown of the power plant is inevitable unless the old stainless steel spent-fuel racks are replaced with "absorber" racks,

Information adapted from: Parisi, L. (Ed.). (1989). *Hot rods: Storage of spent nuclear fuel.* Boulder, CO: Social Science Education Consortium, Inc.

continued

which consist of storage cavities whose walls have three layers—a layer of Boraflex (a neutron-absorbing alloy that allows spent-fuel assemblies to be placed closer together) sandwiched between two layers of stainless steel. Acme proposes at this time to enlarge the capacity of the spent-fuel from its current capacity of 687 to a total of 1,582.

The proposed modification will increase the pool storage capacity to the maximum extent within the confines of the existing pool walls. Acme requests approval to carry out this proposal from the Virginia Energy Agency and from the NRC.

Cancer Patients in Riverton (1994–1995)

Patient and Address	Diagnosis	Age	Date of Diagnosis
1. Betti Paige McFarlane 106 Park Avenue	Colon Cancer	74	July 1994
2. Timothy O'Bryan 106 Park Avenue	Stomach Cancer	68	September 1994
3. Susan Hogge 317 Cedar Lane	Bone Cancer	35	November 1994
4. Sean Pedersen 215 Catesby Jones Dr.	Myelogenous Leukemia	4	January 1995
5. Jenny Pedersen 215 Catesby Jones Dr.	Myelogenous Leukemia	6	July 1995
6. Mathew Jacobs 74 Fern Street	Lung Cancer	49	February 1995
7. Alyssa Anderson 275 Morrison Road	Leukemia	19	April 1995
8. Brian Harper 232 Park Avenue	Prostate Cancer	79	June 1995
9. Julienne Tipins 36 Nettles Lane	Thyroid Cancer	38	August 1995
10. David Montgomery 11 Chapel Road	Bone Cancer	57	June 1995
11. Patricia Higgins 311 Cedar Lane	Breast Cancer	28	September 1994
12. Mary McClosky 216 Park Avenue	Splenic Cancer	81	August 1995
13. Janet Segal 12 Fern Street	Bone Cancer	53	July 1995
14. Paul Miller 300 Park Avenue	Colon Cancer	74	November 1994
15. Helen Roberts 3 Harbor Crescent	Breast Cancer	48	September 1995
16. Joanne Marcus 18 Park Avenue	Breast Cancer	72	March 1995
17. John Gilespi 8 Pine Avenue	Lung Cancer	42	January 1995
18. Paulette Snyder 275 Morrison Rd.	Leukemia	19	April 1994
19. Brad Snyder 205 Morrison Rd.	Skin Cancer	38	September 1995
20. Todd Bristol 15 Park Avenue	Thyroid Nodules	22	December 1994
21. Jason Knott 112 Park Avenue	Esophageal Cancer	71	February 1995

Acme Power Memorandum: Office of the Director

Acme Power
"Pioneers in the Power Industry"
Office of the Director

Memorandum

To: Public Relations Office

From: Don Feldhouse, Director

Date: (date of memo)

Ré: Town Meeting on

These two documents recently came across my desk. It is imperative that the community understand the facts regarding our Maple Island Plant and nuclear power in general before they take action. I would like you to attend the town meeting and be prepared to answer questions regarding how nuclear power is generated and the positive and negative consequences of using nuclear power, as well as the consequences of not using nuclear power.

The policy of this company has been to be completely honest in our presentation of information. I firmly believe that the prejudices many people bring to the nuclear power issue are the consequence of inadequate or faulty information. Please be sure that your presentation presents the facts in a fair and unbiased manner in light of our goal of providing a valuable service to the community.

Newspaper Article, "Silent Holocaust"

By Eugene McLawhon
Danforth Times News Service

Danforth—The worst accident in the history of the Meadowland weapons complex occurred here on November 15, 1989, when a $40 million blaze was started as plutonium ignited. Immediately after the fire, readings revealed radioactivity more than 200 times higher than the normal background level.

It was soon revealed that the Danforth Nuclear Weapons Power Station raged out of control because simple safety upgrades had not been made due to budget constraint. When close inspection of the facility began, huge drums were found stored on-site which leaked oil contaminated with plutonium.

Since the Manhattan Project of the 1940s, nuclear weapons plants have been supervised by lax government regulations. Documents secured by a Meadowland environmental group under the Freedom of Information Act revealed that between 1958 and 1968 the Danforth plant released small but significant amounts of plutonium into the air every day.

Studies of nearby residents show a higher than average rate of leukemia and other cancers. Toxic wastes and radioactivity have been detected in ponds as well as on nearby property. There is concern by health officials about the safety of water supplies in the area.

The details of mismanagement at the Danforth facility are shocking, yet consistent. Recently, Frank Abney, a Danforth plant worker, revealed in testimony before senate investigators that he had been assured that contamination at the work site was at an "acceptable" level.

He stated that he was never advised as to which radioactive substances to avoid on the site. In April 1989, he discovered he was contaminated with plutonium.

"We are living through a 'Silent Holocaust,' and we're tired of being ignored by our government. It's time we stop remediation—the expensive 'undoing' of mistakes. We must have full-scale prevention. Today, more than ever, the administration must begin a restrained path of self-protection."

CAFSE Newspaper Article

Citizen Action Group Protests Nuclear Power Plant

By Terry Gray
Parkland Times News Service

Riverton—Citizens Action for a Safe Environment (CAFSE), a local environmental group, staged a protest in front of Maple Island Nuclear Power Plant on Friday.

Residents of Riverton want to shut down the nuclear power plant after a $785,000 campaign by Acme Power Company failed to overcome arguments based less on environmental and safety issues than on economics.

Many of the citizens were convinced that the Maple Island Plant could not provide electricity to their community at a cost lower than other fuels. In 1989, for example, Riverton's electricity cost was more than twice the cost generated by natural gas.

An important consequence of citizen group action is drawing public attention. The resulting debate concerns the nuclear establishment's attempt to "de-mystify" the processes and human costs of nuclear energy production.

The protest held by CAFSE in Riverton draws focus on other nuclear power facilities in Parkland and throughout the nation. Once touted as the best alternative to oil, nuclear energy's fall from grace began with a nuclear plant disaster at Pennsylvania's Three Mile Island (TMI) in 1979.

Human error as well as equipment failure resulted in the destruction of 70% of TMI's nuclear reactor. Tens of thousands of people were evacuated from the area because of concern over the damaging effect of radioactive emissions released from the plant.

Public confidence in nuclear power was eroded, and the accident resulted in the Nuclear Regulatory Commission's issuing new safety regulations. These anti-nuclear activists declare that no nuclear power plant is completely safe because of the highly radioactive nuclear waste that is a by-product of nuclear power generation.

Others are concerned about the effects of human health and the impact on the individual. CAFSE members point to the possible connection between leukemia and nuclear power emissions.

The CAFSE group has been trying to monitor the incidence of leukemia in the area around the power plant since its opening to determine whether

continued

or not nuclear power emissions are a threat to health and life. "Although the data are not absolutely clear, we think there is a link," said one CAFSE advocate.

A mother's perspective sheds another light on the issue. Barbara Anderson is the mother of 16-year-old Alyssa, who has recently been diagnosed as having leukemia.

Nuclear power advocates, however, are determined to turn nuclear energy's bad reputation around in the 1990s. Their renewed efforts have revived

the debate over nuclear power's role in America's energy future. Supporters believe that nuclear power is an ideal source of electricity.

They argue that nuclear plants could help reduce America's dependency on foreign oil because uranium ore, the fuel source used in nuclear fission, is widely distributed throughout the United States. They contend that this dependency on foreign oil is brought even more into focus in the wake of the Persian Gulf War. "We've just witnessed the greatest reason for not importing oil," says Janet Alexander, media director of the U.S. Council of Energy Awareness, a pro-nuclear power industry group.

But critics of nuclear power note that only about 5% of U.S. electricity is currently generated by oil today, compared with 18% in 1973. Most oil consumption goes for transportation, not the generation of electricity! Thus, creating more nuclear power plants may produce more electricity, but it would do little to reduce America's dependence on oil.

Nevertheless, proponents of nuclear power claim that oil and coal produce dangerous emissions that pollute the atmosphere. Nuclear energy is a cleaner source of power because it does not emit such gases, they say.

Anti-nuclear activists vehemently disagree. The residents demonstrating in the Citizens Action for a Safe Environment protest are anxious for the Maple Island Nuclear Power Company to get rid of the radioactive waste elsewhere. They fear a "core meltdown" or other tragic accident associated with the nuclear facility.

By focusing attention on the nuclear waste issue, the group plans to expose ACME's possible "covert operations" concerning cover-up of plant problems/accidents for the past years. Their protest heightens public awareness concerning such possibilities.

These citizens recognize that the safe disposal of high-level waste remains a difficult, and perhaps unsolveable, problem for the nuclear industry. They are aware that efforts to find a permanent repository for nuclear waste have been fiercely opposed by residents of the areas being considered. There is a strong cry of "Not in my backyard!" (NIMBY Syndrome) throughout the nation.

Nuclear industry advocates remain optimistic as they point to the Bush administration's recent show of support for nuclear power in

continued

its long-awaited national energy strategy. They note that other nations such as Britain, Japan, Germany, and South Korea rely on nuclear power to supply a significant percentage of their energy production. More than 70% of France's electricity is generated by nuclear power.

Yet, the citizens of Riverton indicate in their protest that the possibility of an accident at Maple Island facility is a reality they want to bring to the attention of the public. They point to the accident at Japan's Mihama nuclear power plant of February 9 of this year. This, they say, reminds the public that no country is immune from the threat of nuclear disaster.

Name _____ Date _____

Acme Power Memorandum:
Department of Waste Management

Acme Power
"Pioneers in the Power Industry"
Department of Waste Management

Memorandum

To: Office of Mayor Christine Barrett

From: Jerry Brown, Vice President of Waste Management

Date:

Re: Expanding Waste Disposal Capacity

We at the Maple Island Nuclear Power Plant foresee the need to expand our on-site waste disposal capacity in the near future. In the past, there has been much discussion and opposition to expanding our waste storage facilities. For your information, I have provided a short history of our waste disposal capabilities.

When the Maple Island Nuclear Power Plant was constructed in 1970, Acme Power Company intended to store spent nuclear fuel "on site" until a permanent repository was provided by the U.S. Department of Energy. Initially, two spent-fuel pools provided the capacity to store 210 fuel assemblies. In the mid-1980s, it became apparent that the repository proposed by the U.S. Department of Energy in the Nuclear Waste Policy Act of 1982 would not be operational in time to dispose of the spent fuel from the Maple Island plant. Consequently, a modification project was initiated in 1984 to increase the pool storage capacity from 210 fuel assemblies to 678 assemblies. Now we see the need to expand the capacity to 1,582 assemblies to keep the plant operational.

Due to Local Ordinance 829-85, we need to gain the approval of the mayor and council before implementing any new expansion or addition of waste facilities within the jurisdiction of the City of Riverton. We ask for your approval in a timely fashion. Thank you.

Name _____   Date _____

City of Riverton Ordinance 829-85 and Amendment

The City of Riverton
City of Good Tidings
Office of the Mayor

Local Ordinance 829-85 (Adopted August 15, 1985)

All businesses, industries, nonprofit organizations, and/or living complexes must apply for approval through the mayor's office before beginning any expansions, additions, or formations of waste disposal sites within the jurisdiction of the City of Riverton. This includes garbage disposal, human waste, hospital waste, low- and high-grade nuclear waste, and any other waste products known to be hazardous or potentially hazardous to the citizens of Riverton. Failure to comply could result in fines of a minimum of $1,000 with *no* upper limit.

Amendment to Local Ordinance 829-85 (Adopted September 15, 1987)

In addition to the preset conditions to L.O. 829-85, the parties responsible for obtaining permission are extended to include local, state, and federal government agencies, as well as religious institutions and school districts. The town council has the right to call for a special review of any request accepted or denied by the mayor regarding L.O. 829-85.

Memo to the Mayor

Memo

To: Mayor Christine Barrett

From: Congressman Paul Greene

Date:

Subject: **Maple Island Power Plant**

I have received letters from the environmental group, CAFSE, complaining about safety concerns at Maple Island. However, I have also received letters from power plant employees who are concerned about losing their jobs.

I think you can resolve this controversy better than I can, because you are closer to all the parties involved and have easier access to the data from the plant. I will support your decision at the national level.

An Inside Look at Nuclear Power Plants

4A

Instructional Purpose

• To provide an opportunity for students to visit a nuclear power facility (See Optional Lesson 4B for possible alternative.)

Curriculum Alignment  **Goal 1** Concept  **Goal 2** Content ○ **Goal 3** Process/ Experimental Design ○ **Goal 4** Process/ Reasoning

Lesson Length

Two 60-minute sessions

 ## Session 1 Activities

1. Review the **Need to Know Board** for questions that still need to be answered.

2. Brainstorm a list of questions students would like to have answered on the field trip.

3. Assign responsibilities for obtaining various kinds of information to different students.

4. Ask students for a list of things they particularly want to see if it is possible.

5. **Ask:**
   • What questions would you like answered during our field trip?

   • Can you think of specific things an energy consultant would look for or ask?

   • What about an anti-nuclear activist?

   • What should you be looking for or asking of the people at the plant?

   • How can we ask these questions in nonoffensive ways?

 ## Session 2 Activities

1. Students visit a local nuclear power plant.

2. Hold a debriefing session regarding the field trip. Review the **Need to Know Board,** removing questions that have been answered and adding new issues, if necessary. Synthesize new information with the existing database.

Extending Student Learning

- Have students research the nuclear power facilities located in the United States and in other parts of the world.

 Assessment

- Class discussion participation
- Nature and quality of questions asked at the field trip site

 Technology Integration

- Students can develop a webpage to show others what they learned during their tour of the nuclear power plant. They may want to create a "virtual tour" of a simulated nuclear power plant. (Webpages should not include possibly sensitive details about the plant they visited, for security purposes.)
- If neither a field trip nor a guest speaker can be arranged, students can interview a nuclear power professional online using e-mail or a messaging program.

Guest Speaker (Optional)

4B

Instructional Purpose

- To provide an opportunity for students to engage in a dialogue with an individual who works in a nuclear power plant

Curriculum Alignment

 **Goal 1** Concept  **Goal 2** Content  Goal 3 Process/ Experimental Design  Goal 4 Process/ Reasoning

 Materials/Resources

- Visitor Planning Sheet (Handout 4B.1)
- Problem Log Questions (Handout 4B.2)
- Problem Log Questions (Handout 4B.3)

Lesson Length

Three 60-minute sessions

 Session 1 Activities

1. Help students select which items from the **Need to Know Board** might be best answered by the guest speaker. Brainstorm other questions. (The "best" questions to ask will, of course, depend on the area of expertise of the guest speaker.)

2. Sort questions into most and least important. Students should also be encouraged to think about the best way to phrase the questions. Are they specific enough? Are they too specific? A core list of questions can be recorded on a chart or on the board. Students can then add any of their own questions to individual **Visitor Planning Sheets** (Handout 4B.1).

3. **Ask:**
   - What information do we want to know about the nuclear power system?
   - What information will the guest speaker be most qualified to give?
   - What do we want to know by the time the guest speaker leaves?

- What facts do we want to get from this person that might help us with the Maple Island problem?
- Which of these questions are most important?
- How can we get an idea of this person's perspective on this kind of situation?
- Do you think this person will have a bias? What would it be? How can we find out?

 ## Session 2 Activity

1. *Guest Speaker.* The guest provides his/her information about nuclear power. Students take notes and ask their questions to the guest speaker. Students should also be prepared to share with the guest speaker background on the problem and their actions to date.
2. Have students answer **Problem Log Questions** (Handout 4B.2)

 ## Session 3 Activities

1. Analyze the information from the guest speaker. In a follow-up to the guest speaker session, teacher and students should review the **Need to Know Board,** removing questions that have been answered and adding new issues, if necessary. Synthesize new information with the existing database.
2. Teachers and students should discuss the potential bias in the information provided by the guest speaker and the possible effects of that bias on the validity of the information.
3. **Ask:**
   - What were the things we learned from the guest speaker?
   - How does the new information affect our thinking about the problem?
   - Do we need to reorganize our approach to the problem?
   - Did this person reveal a particular bias? If so, what?
   - Where can we go to get another perspective? A balanced report of information?
4. Have students answer **Problem Log Questions** (Handout 4B.3)

 ## Assessment

- Record of new information in **Problem Logs** based on the guest speaker's presentation
- Reflection on bias in the **Problem Logs**
- Thank-you letter to the guest speaker, describing which information was particularly helpful

Name _____ Date _____

Visitor Planning Sheet

Name of Visitor: _____

Who is this visitor?

_____

_____

Why is this visitor coming to see us?

_____

_____

Why is this visitor important to us?

_____

_____

_____

What would you like to tell our visitor about our problem?

_____

_____

_____

What questions do you want to ask the visitor?

_____

_____

_____

Problem Log Questions

Can bias be prevented or is a person always biased to some degree? What strategies do you think would be helpful to offset our own biases?

Problem Log Questions

Take just a minute to think about the problem itself. What does the problem look like now compared to what it was at the beginning of this lesson? How has it changed? What has surprised you about this problem?

Nuclear Reactions

5

Instructional Purpose

- To introduce experimental design in a relevant context
- To introduce the nuclear fission process and explain how the process generates energy
- To introduce radioisotopes and radioactive decay (alpha, beta, and gamma decay)
- To allow students to construct a mental model of a chain reaction

---

Curriculum Alignment

 Goal 1
Concept

 Goal 2
Content

 Goal 3
Process/
Experimental Design

 Goal 4
Process/
Reasoning

 Vocabulary

Alpha Particle The positively charged particle emitted in the radioactive decay of certain radioactive atoms. An alpha particle is identical to the nucleus of the helium atom.

Atom The smallest part of a chemical element that has all the chemical properties of that element

Beta Particle It is smaller than an alpha particle. A beta particle can pass through paper but may be stopped by glass such as that found in windows.

Constant The factor or factors in an experiment that are kept the same and not allowed to vary

Control The part of an experiment that serves as a standard of comparison. A control is used to detect the effects of factors that should be kept constant, but that vary.

Decay Product The isotope produced by the decay of a radioactive isotope

Dependent Variable The factor or variable that may change as a result of changes purposely made in the independent variable

Electron A subatomic particle with a negative charge. The electron circles the nucleus of an atom.

Fission Splitting apart atoms with the result that large amounts of energy and one or more neutrons are released. The splitting of a nucleus into two lighter nuclei, accompanied by the emission of two or more neutrons and a significant amount of energy. Fission in a nuclear reactor is initiated by the nucleus absorbing a neutron. Nuclear power plants split the nuclei of uranium atoms.

Gamma Rays Waves of electromagnetic energy that are very penetrating and are best shielded by lead; they are emitted during the decay of certain radioactive materials

Hypothesis A tentative explanation for an observation, phenomenon, or scientific problem that can be tested by further investigation

Independent Variable The variable that is changed on purpose by the experimenter

Neutron A subatomic particle that appears in the nucleus of all atoms except hydrogen. Neutrons have no electrical charge.

Nuclear Chain Reaction In a nuclear chain reaction, a fissionable nucleus absorbs a neutron and splits into two smaller, nearly equal nuclei, releasing additional neutrons. These in turn can be absorbed by other fissionable nuclei, releasing still more neutrons. This gives rise to a self-sustaining reaction.

Nuclear Radiation Ionizing radiation (alpha, beta, and gamma) originating in the nuclei of radioactive atoms

Nuclear Waste Radioactive by-products from any activity, including energy production, weapons production, and medical treatment and research

Nucleus The central part of an atom that contains the protons and neutrons

Proton A subatomic particle in the nucleus of an atom with about the same mass as the neutron but carrying a positive charge

Radiation Energy emitted in the form of rays or particles that are potentially harmful to humans; it moves through space in the form of particles or electromagnetic waves

Radioactive A property of some materials whereby spontaneous emissions of alpha or beta particles or gamma rays occur; these particles and rays are potentially harmful to humans.

Radioactive Decay The process by which radioactive materials become less radioactive over time

Radioactivity The property possessed by some elements, such as uranium, of spontaneously emitting alpha or beta particles or gamma rays

Radioisotope A radioactive isotope of a chemical element. Radioisotopes may occur naturally, or they may be artificially created from normal isotopes of an element.

Reactor A large machine that heats water

Materials/Resources

- Periodic Table of the Elements
- Dominoes (100 or more)
- Large table or floor space
- Stopwatch
- Nuclear Fission (Handout 5.1)
- Nuclear Decay Discussion Questions (Handout 5.2)
- Nuclear Decay Discussion Questions—Answer Protocol (Teacher Resource 1)
- Problem Log Questions (Handout 5.3)
- Student Brainstorming Guide (Handout 5.4)
- Experimental Design Planner (Handout 5.5)
- Experimental Protocol (Handout 5.6)
- Laboratory Report (Handout 5.7)
- Sample Protocol Problem Log Questions (Handout 5.8)
- Problem Log Questions (Handout 5.9)
- Ping-Pong Decay Worksheet (Handout 5.10)
- Ping-Pong Decay Worksheet Possible Responses (Teacher Resource 2)
- Problem Log Questions (Handout 5.11)

Lesson Length

Three 60-minute sessions

 Session 1 Activities

1. Divide the class into small groups and distribute **Nuclear Fission** (Handout 5.1). Have students read the information, individually respond to the short-answer questions, and discuss their answers within their group. Make sure each group comes to a consensus on each question.

2. Bring the class back into the large group and discuss the question in relation to the **Need to Know Board.**

3. Talk about radiation and what forms it might take. Discuss radioactive decay in terms of the problem. Be sure to mention half-life and disposal of waste materials.

4. Have the students consider what happens to the stable uranium-238 during nuclear power production. Does it remain unchanged?

5. Once again, divide the class into small groups and distribute **Nuclear Decay Discussion Questions** (Handout 5.2). Discuss questions and have them read the passage and analyze the decay reactions that follow.

6. Bring the class back into the large group to process the connections between the **Need to Know Board,** and the discussion.

7. **Ask:**
   - What is the importance of fission to the nuclear power plant?
   - What do we know about fission?
   - What have we found out about fission as it relates to power production?
   - What is radioactive decay? How does it relate to our problem?
   - Are there many types of radioactive decay?
   - What is the importance of radioactive decay to our problem?

8. Have students complete **Problem Log Questions** (Handout 5.3).

Assessment

- Completed **Problem Log Questions**
- Completed small-group discussion handouts

Extending Student Learning

- Have students discuss nuclear fusion and how the sun produces nuclear energy.

Technology Integration

- Students may use the Internet to research any of the issues discussed thus far.
- Students may use spreadsheet software to develop a chart or graph showing the states and/or countries that have nuclear power plants.

Session 2 Activities

1. Review the **Need to Know Board** and discuss nuclear chain reactions. Nuclear chain reactions are an important consideration in power plant design as well as in the safe handling of any radioactive substance.

2. Discuss ways to show how nuclear chain reactions work. Discuss how transmission of a disease can be seen as a chain reaction. Use the following example:

   Scenario statement. Imagine that you come to school one day with a common cold. That day you transmit your cold germs to two other people; they in turn give it to two others who in turn do the same. Before you know it, everyone in school is sneezing. You have set off a chain reaction. Similarly, electrons in a photomultiplier tube in an electronic instrument multiply in a chain reaction so that a tiny input produces a huge output. When one neutron triggers the release of two or more neutrons in a piece of uranium and the triggered neutrons trigger others in a chain reaction, the results can be devastating.

3. Show students the materials for the lesson. Divide the students into small groups and ask them to develop a method for modeling the rates of chain reactions using dominoes. To prompt students for the brainstorming activity, refer to the questions in the following "Ask" section. Pass out a copy of the **Student Brainstorming Guide** (Handout 5.4) and have students complete it.

4. Discuss the brainstorming results as a class.

5. Distribute copies of the **Experimental Design Planner** (Handout 5.5). If this is the first time students have seen it, have the class complete it together and explain the meaning of each of the terms.

6. After they have completed the **Experimental Design Planner** (Handout 5.5), have each group write its protocol on the **Experimental Protocol** (Handout 5.6). They should include every step they plan to take, the materials they will use, and a data table to record their data. Students should also indicate what safety procedures they plan to use as a part of the overall experimental design.

7. Have students either work individually or in small groups to conduct the experiment. When they have finished, have them complete the **Laboratory Report** (Handout 5.7).

8. After students perform their experiments, bring the groups together to discuss their results, limitations of the results, and possible revisions in experimental design. Complete **Sample Protocol Problem Log Questions** (Handout 5.8) or a version that matches the experiment that students did.

9. Have students complete **Problem Log Questions** (Handout 5.9).

10. **Ask:**

   • What do you think a chain reaction is?

   • How could you demonstrate this with dominoes?

   • Would the rate of the reaction change if we changed the spacing between dominoes?

   • Would the rate of the reaction change if we changed the arrangement of dominoes?

Sample Protocol

1. Set up a string of dominoes with each pair about half a domino length apart in a straight line. Push the first domino, and measure how long it takes for the entire string to fall over using the stopwatch.

2. Do it again! Arrange an equal number of dominoes in a straight line about half a domino apart. Push the first domino over and calculate the rate at which the dominoes fall. Is this rate constant over time?

3. Next, arrange the same number of dominoes in a pattern as shown in Figure 5.1. Push the first domino, and measure how long it takes for the

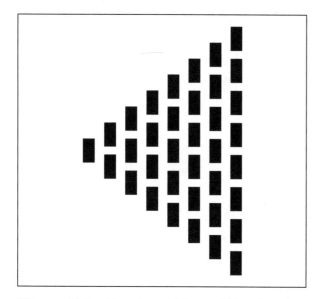

Note: Each row of dominoes is spaced about half a domino length apart just as in Step 1.

Note: Arrange the same number of dominoes in the pyramid pattern shown to the left as arranged in the straight line in Step 1 and Step 2. For example, if 100 dominoes are set up in a straight line in Step 1 and Step 2, then set up 100 dominoes in the pyramid pattern shown for Step 3 and Step 4.

Figure 5.1 Overhead View of Domino Arrangement

entire string to fall over using the stopwatch. Compare this time to the time in Step 1's configuration.

4. Once again, arrange the dominoes in a pattern as shown in Figure 5.1. Push the first domino over to calculate the rate at which the dominoes fall. To do this, have one student run the stopwatch and call out the seconds. Other students mark down which row of dominoes falls when the second is called out. The rate can be calculated by counting the number of dominoes that fell during each second separately. How do the rates in Step 2 compare to the rates found in this step?

 Assessment

1. Completed **Problem Logs**
2. Completed **Laboratory Reports**
3. Completed **Sample Protocol Problem Log Questions**

 Session 3 Activities

1. At a time when students have begun to investigate radioactive decay, gather them together and have students summarize what they have learned.

2. Tell students that there is an important radioactive decay process that is the basis for nuclear power plant operations, namely:

$$_{92}U^{235} + n \rightarrow {_{36}}Kr^{90} + {_{56}}Ba^{142} + 4\,n$$

Because four neutrons are released for every neutron consumed, the reaction is self-sustaining—it begins with a single neutron, which reacts and produces four neutrons, which react and produce sixteen, and so on.

3. Ask students to imagine the following (a model originally suggested by Richard P. Feynman, a noted physicist):

> Think of each unstable uranium-235 atom as a mousetrap that has been set with a ping-pong ball balanced on top. If the mousetrap is sprung, the ping-pong ball will fly off: the ping-pong ball acts like the neutron that is released during radioactive decay. (Obviously, this is not a perfectly homologous picture—but it's hard to imagine a mousetrap with four ping-pong balls balanced on top.)

Once they have this mental picture, divide them into small groups and ask them to complete the **Ping-Pong Decay Worksheet** (Handout 5.10).

4. After discussion of the **Ping-Pong Decay Worksheet** (Handout 5.10), have students complete **Problem Log Questions** (Handout 5.11).

Assessment

- Completed **Ping-Pong Decay Worksheet**

Extending Student Learning

- Have students set up a physical model of a nuclear chain reaction, or have them write a computer program to model this process.

Nuclear Fission

When an atom of the radioactive isotope uranium-235 is bombarded by neutrons, it is possible for the atomic nucleus to absorb one of the "incoming" neutrons. The resultant and highly unstable uranium-236 nucleus tends to split (hence, nuclear fission) forming the nuclei of two new elements—barium and krypton, for example—at the same time releasing two or three high-energy neutrons and a large amount of energy (approximately 300 billion joules). If this process is controlled so that one of the released neutrons itself bombards and is absorbed by another uranium-235 nucleus, a chain reaction results that can produce large amounts of energy converted to heat.

This is exactly what happens inside a nuclear reactor. Naturally occurring uranium contains about 99.3 percent of stable uranium-238 and 0.7 percent of radioactive uranium-235, a mixture that will not sustain a chain reaction. U-235 can be enriched, however, so that the fuel rods in a nuclear reactor contain 97 percent of U-238 and 3 percent of U-235. These fuel rods are sheathed in graphite to slow down the movement of the bombarding neutrons, thereby increasing the chances of absorption of neutrons by the U-235 nuclei. In addition, rods of boron steel can be lowered into the reactor to absorb neutrons if the reaction is proceeding too fast.

1. Are all the 300 billion joules produced by a *single* fission reaction converted into heat? What forms could the emergent energy take? Explain your answer.

2. What possible explanations are there for the reason that naturally occurring uranium does *not* produce nuclear chain reactions?

3. What reasons can you give for slowing neutrons down to allow for better absorption rates?

4. What are the possible outcomes of a nuclear reactor that is proceeding too fast and is *not* checked by the boron steel?

Nuclear Decay Discussion Questions

Directions: Read the following passage and respond collaboratively to the questions. Refer to the periodic table of the elements when necessary.

In decaying, an isotope may:

- Lose positively charged particles from the atomic nuclei (alpha particles). Because of the resulting loss of atomic mass, this has the effect of converting the original element into one that is placed earlier in the periodic table. An example of alpha decay is the natural decay of uranium, which, through a number of conversions, eventually decays to form lead.

- Lose negatively charged electrons (beta particles). This occurs as the result of a nuclear neutron becoming a proton, and the effect is to move the element "up" the periodic table. An example of beta decay is the decay of carbon-14 to nitrogen, a process that takes many thousands of years and that is used in the accurate dating of organic remains.

- Emit, as high energy electromagnetic waves, the highly penetrating (and therefore potentially damaging) gamma rays, which have no electric charge.

1. Analyze the following decay reaction:

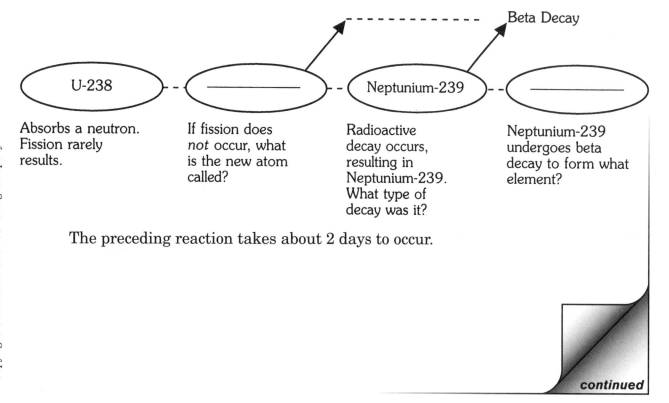

The preceding reaction takes about 2 days to occur.

continued

2. Analyze the following decay reaction:

Beta Decay   2-Alpha Decays

Thorium-232 - - Radium-228 - - Actinium-228 - - (⎯⎯⎯) - - (- - - - - -)

3. What implications does this have on radioactive waste from a nuclear reaction, if any?

Nuclear Decay Discussion
Questions—Answer Protocol
(Teacher Resource 1)

Directions: Read the following passage and respond collaboratively to the questions. Refer to the periodic table of the elements when necessary.

In decaying, an isotope may:

- Lose positively charged particles from the atomic nuclei (alpha particles). Because of the resulting loss of atomic mass, this has the effect of converting the original element into one that is placed earlier in the periodic table. An example of alpha decay is the natural decay of uranium, which, through a number of conversions, eventually decays to form lead.

- Lose negatively charged electrons (beta particles). This occurs as the result of a nuclear neutron becoming a proton, and the effect is to move the element "up" the periodic table. An example of beta decay is the decay of carbon-14 to nitrogen, a process that takes many thousands of years and that is used in the accurate dating of organic remains.

- Emit, as high energy electromagnetic waves, the highly penetrating (and therefore potentially damaging) gamma rays, which have no electric charge.

1. Analyze the following decay reaction:

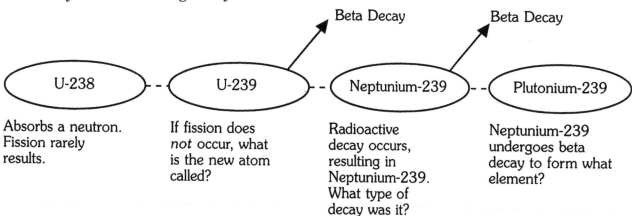

The preceding reaction takes about 2 days to occur.

2. Analyze the following decay reaction:

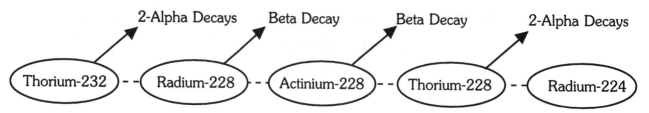

3. What implications does this have on radioactive waste from a nuclear reaction, if any?

3. How can we use these materials to help us find out?

4. What do we think will happen? (What is our hypothesis?)

5. What will we need to observe or measure in order to find out the answer to our scientific question?

Experimental Design Planner

Title:

_____

Hypothesis (educated guess about what will happen):

_____

Independent variable (the variable that you change):

_____

Dependent variable (the variable that responds to changes in the independent variable):

_____

Observations/Measurements:

_____

Constants (all the things or factors that remain the same):

_____

Control (the standard for comparing experimental effects):

Name _____   Date _____

Experimental Protocol

1. List the materials you will need.

2. Write a step-by-step description of what you will do (like a recipe!). List every action you will take during the experiment.

continued

3. What data will you be collecting?

4. Design a data table to collect and analyze your information.

Name _____   Date _____

Laboratory Report

1. What did you do or test? (Include your experiment title.)

2. How did you do it? Cite materials and methods. You can go back to your **Experimental Protocol** (Handout 5.6) and use the information from the first two questions.

3. What did you find out? (Include a data summary and the explanation of its meaning.)

continued

4. What did you learn from your experiment?

5. What additional questions do you now have?

6. Does the information you learned help with the problem?

Name   Date

Sample Protocol Problem Log Questions

1. Which reaction set-up took a shorter time to knock over all the dominoes? Why?

2. Describe how the number of dominoes being knocked over per second changes in each reaction type.

3. Imagine that the dominoes are neutrons released by uranium atoms when they fission. Neutrons from the nucleus of each fissioning uranium atom hit other uranium atoms and cause them to fission. In a complete paragraph, compare and contrast the domino reactions to a nuclear chain reaction.

Problem Log Questions

1. How has the problem changed now that you have developed an idea of a chain reaction?

2. What do you think is the next step in addressing the problem? Why?

Name _____ Date _____

Ping-Pong Decay Worksheet

1. What would happen if you had a single ping-pong-ball-mousetrap combination set up in the middle of an otherwise empty room and it spontaneously "decayed," releasing its ping-pong ball at high speed?

2. What if you had a single ping-pong-ball-mousetrap set up in the middle of a group of unset, ordinary mousetraps and it suddenly "decayed"?

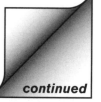

continued

3. What would happen if you had a room full of ping-pong-ball-mousetrap set-ups placed at 1-foot intervals and one of them spontaneously "decayed," releasing its ping-pong ball at high speed?

4. Which of the three experiments described in Question 1 through Question 3 is a good model for a nuclear chain reaction? Why?

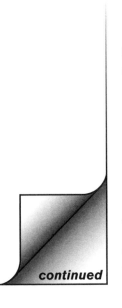

continued

5. "Critical mass" is the term that describes the smallest amount of a radioactive material needed to set off a spontaneous chain reaction. How could you find out what the critical mass of ping-pong-ball-mousetrap set-ups would be? What factors would you have to consider?

6. Critical density is the fraction of the atoms that need to be unstable in order for the material to be able to sustain a chain reaction. How could you use the ping-pong-ball-mousetrap set-up to model critical density?

7. Moderators are substances that absorb neutrons and prevent them from causing any more radioactive decays. How could you model the action of a moderator in the ping-pong-ball-mousetrap experiment?

Teacher Ping-Pong Decay
Worksheet Possible Responses
(Teacher Resource 2)

1. What would happen if you had a single ping-pong-ball-mousetrap combination set-up in the middle of an otherwise empty room and it spontaneously "decayed," releasing its ping-pong ball at high speed?

   Answer: *You'd have a sprung mousetrap and a ping-pong ball.*

2. What if you had a single ping-pong-ball-mousetrap set-up in the middle of a group of unset, ordinary mousetraps and it suddenly "decayed"?

   Answer: *You'd have one more sprung mousetrap to add to the collection, plus a bouncing ping-pong ball that would eventually come to rest.*

3. What would happen if you had a room full of ping-pong-ball-mousetrap set-ups placed at 1-foot intervals and one of them spontaneously "decayed," releasing its ping-pong ball at high speed?

   Answer: *The first Ping-Pong ball would probably bounce onto another setup, causing it to decay. This process would repeat itself and you would have a chain reaction that would result in the decay of most (if not all) of the set-ups in the room.*

4. Which of the three experiments described in questions 1–3 is a good model for a nuclear chain reaction? Why?

   Answer: *Question 3*

5. "Critical mass" is the term that describes the smallest amount of a radioactive material needed to set off a spontaneous chain reaction. How could you find out what the critical mass of ping-pong-ball-mousetrap set-ups would be? What factors would you have to consider?

   Answer: *You'd have to test and see; factors to consider would be the hardness of the floor and walls, which would affect the ability of the balls to bounce; the existence or nonexistence of floors and ceiling; the shape of the array of mousetraps; the spacing of the mousetraps from each other; the number of ping-pong balls released as each set-up decays . . . and so on.*

6. Critical density is the fraction of the atoms that need to be unstable in order for the material to be able to sustain a chain reaction. How could you use the ping-pong-ball-mousetrap set-up to model critical density?

Answer: *You could model it experimentally, using a combination of sprung mousetraps and ping-pong ball set-ups and gradually increasing the number of set-ups.*

7. Moderators are substances that absorb neutrons and prevent them from causing any more radioactive decays. How could you model the action of a moderator in the ping-pong-ball-mousetrap experiment?

Answer: *One way would be to add boxes full of something that would stop ping-pong balls that landed in them from bouncing. Enough of these boxes spaced at regular intervals should be able to reduce the intensity of the chain reaction or stop it altogether.*

Name _____   Date _____

Problem Log Questions

1. Think about what you have learned about systems and apply that knowledge to nuclear reactions.

2. Which systems are involved in nuclear reactions?

continued

3. Draw a diagram of one of the systems within nuclear reactions. Label all parts of the system in terms of its boundaries, elements, inputs, outputs, and interactions.

4. What safety issues emerge when you think of your nuclear system interactions?

Nuclear Reactors

6

Instructional Purpose

• To understand where and how nuclear fission occurs within a nuclear power plant

Curriculum Alignment Goal 1 Concept Goal 2 Content Goal 3 Process/ Experimental Design ○Goal 4 Process/ Reasoning

 Vocabulary

Control Rod Rods that slide up and down in between the fuel assemblies in order to control the speed of the nuclear reaction; these rods contain cadmium and boron, two elements that absorb neutrons but do not fission. These rods act as sponges to absorb neutrons that might hit other uranium atoms and cause them to split.

Fission Splitting apart atoms with the result that large amounts of energy and one or more neutrons are released. Nuclear power plants split the nuclei of uranium atoms.

Fuel Assembly Bound fuel rods containing uranium pellets that generate heat; a fuel assembly usually consists of approximately 240 fuel rods that are about 20 feet long and contain 200 fuel pellets.

Pressure Vessel The large container that surrounds and protects the reactor core; a pressure vessel's walls can be as thick as 9 inches and it can weigh up to 300 tons

Reactor A large machine that heats water

Water Coolant Usually purified water, the coolant keeps the temperature at a low enough level that it will not damage the core

 Materials/Resources

• Prepared envelopes containing strips of paper, cut from Steps in Producing Nuclear Power

• Steps in Producing Nuclear Power (Teacher Resource 1)

- Problem Log Questions (Handout 6.1)
- Aluminum baking pan
- Long kitchen matches (one for each group)
- Box of birthday candles (twenty-five for the first trial, up to fifteen for the second trial, for each group)
- Modeling clay
- Ruler
- Stopwatch
- Goggles

Lesson Length

60 minutes

 ## Activities

1. Tell students that nuclear fission takes place in a reactor within a nuclear power plant. Tell students that a nuclear reactor is basically a machine that heats water. Display the word *reactor* and its definition on the chalkboard; ask students to copy the definition into the section of their **Problem Logs** that is reserved for key words and phrases.

2. Explain to students that the core of a nuclear reactor has four main parts: the fuel assemblies, the control rods, the coolant or moderator, and the pressure vessel. Have students copy the definitions into the section of their **Problem Logs** that is reserved for key words and phrases.

3. Have students make a sketch in their **Problem Logs** of a nuclear reactor. Have them label the control rods, fuel assembly, water coolant, and pressure vessel. Once students have attempted this sketch, ask them to visit http://people.howstuffworks.com/nuclear-power3.htm ("How Nuclear Power Works") to check their sketches.

4. Have students use the site to read about how nuclear power works, with the goal that they will be able to understand the steps in producing nuclear power.

5. Divide students into groups of three or four. Distribute prepared envelopes to students. Use **Steps in Producing Nuclear Power** (Teacher Resource 1). Ask students to sequence the strips from their envelopes into the correct order. Have student groups prepare a written statement justifying the manner in which they sequenced the steps.

6. Have each student group report on its chosen sequence and the manner in which group members justified it. Have other groups comment on the reporting group's reasons for sequencing the steps.

7. Ask students why it might be important to control the speed of the nuclear reaction. (*Controlling the speed might slow down or speed up the rate at which atoms fission and release their energy. It would be useful to be able to control the speed at times when different amounts of electricity need to be generated.*)

8. In small groups, ask students to cover the bottom of an aluminum baking pan with a layer of clay at least 2 inches thick. Then ask them to arrange twenty-five matches side by side leaving at least a quarter of an inch between matches.

9. Have students light the first match and measure the amount of time it takes for all of the matches to light and burn out.

10. Have students record this time in data tables in their **Problem Logs.** Emphasize to students that what they just observed was a *chain reaction.* This is what happens when neutrons escape the nucleus during fission. Neutrons seek to bombard other nuclei and repeat the process over and over again.

11. Next, have students clear the burnt matches out of their aluminum baking pans, leaving the clay in place in the bottom of the pan.

12. For the next set-up, have students arrange candles and matches side by side in the aluminum baking pan, alternating candles and matches. They should remember to leave at least one-quarter of an inch between the candles and matches.

13. Have students light the first match and measure the amount of time it takes for all of the matches to ignite and then burn out. Have students record this time in data tables in their **Problem Logs.**

14. Have students make a comparison between the two times they recorded and then generate a conclusion for the difference in times. (*The candles slow down the rate at which the matches ignite and release energy.*) Discuss their responses.

15. Have students complete **Problem Log Questions** (Handout 6.1).

🍎 Note

- This experiment produces quite a bit of smoke and should be conducted in a well-ventilated room or laboratory. Teachers might want to consider demonstrating this experiment rather than having groups of students conduct it, although it is a valuable experience for students.

Assessment

- Evaluate student group work on sequencing the production of nuclear power.
- Using the set of generalizations for systems (see Lesson 2), have students describe one aspect of the production of nuclear power in relation to one or more generalizations.
- Completed **Problem Log Questions**

Technology Integration

- Encourage students to participate in a simulation on nuclear energy at the National Regulatory Commission website. At http://www.nrc.gov/reading-rm/basic-ref/teachers/unit3.html, students can simulate running a nuclear power plant.

Steps in Producing Nuclear Power
(Teacher Resource 1)

Reproduce this page as many times as needed. Cut the page into strips and put the strips into an envelope, making sure that they are randomly ordered. Each group should receive one envelope.

Collect mildly enriched uranium.
Form the uranium into pellets.
Insert pellets into long rods and bundle the rods together to form bundles.
Insert the bundles inside a pressure vessel filled with water.
Add control rods made of a material that absorbs neutrons and that can be raised and lowered to control the speed of the nuclear reaction.
Allow the uranium bundles to heat the water and create steam.
Watch the steam drive a turbine.
Watch the turbine spin a generator to produce power.

1. Collect mildly enriched uranium.

2. Form the uranium into pellets.

3. Insert pellets into long rods and bundle the rods together to form bundles.

4. Insert the bundles inside a pressure vessel filled with water.

5. Add control rods made of a material that absorbs neutrons and that can be raised and lowered to control the speed of the nuclear reaction.

6. Allow the uranium bundles to heat the water and create steam.

7. Watch the steam drive a turbine.

8. Watch the turbine spin a generator to produce power.

Problem Log Questions

1. Can a nuclear reactor be considered a system? Explain using systems vocabulary and systems generalizations.

2. Based on the experiment conducted in class today, can you think of any other way to slow down the speed at which the matches burn?

continued

3. Based on what you now know about nuclear reactors, what do you perceive as potential problems in using nuclear energy to create electricity?

4. What are some possible steps you might take to overcome these potential problems?

Modeling Fission

7

Instructional Purpose

- To understand the outcomes of splitting an atom
- To investigate the effects of force exerted on a model atom
- To describe the events that occur during nuclear fission

Curriculum Alignment Goal 1 **Concept** Goal 2 **Content** Goal 3 **Process/ Experimental Design** ◯Goal 4 **Process/ Reasoning**

Vocabulary

Fission A nuclear reaction in which an atomic nucleus splits into fragments releasing massive amounts of energy

Materials/Resources

- Small water glass that has been marked with a grease pencil on the outside at the two-thirds-full level
- Grease pencil
- Six ounces rubbing alcohol
- Cooking oil
- Water
- Teaspoon
- Cream cheese or dip spreader (or similar dull knife)
- Paper towels

- Systems Diagram (Handout 7.1)
- Systems Diagram: Suggested Responses (Teacher Resource 1)
- Problem Log Questions (Handout 7.2)

Lesson Length

60 minutes

Activities

1. In small groups, ask students to review the definition of fission by having them explain the process to each other in their own words.

2. Have student work groups examine the premarked glass. Explain to them that it has been marked so that they will

not overfill the glass. Have students select a group member to fill the water glass half full with rubbing alcohol. Have student work groups select another member to add enough water so that the glass is two-thirds full (up to the grease pencil mark). Have groups select a third member to stir the alcohol/water mixture thoroughly with the teaspoon. After the mixture has been thoroughly stirred, ask the same student to dry the teaspoon using the paper towels provided. Have the fourth member of the group pour cooking oil into the teaspoon and then hold the spoon containing the cooking oil just over the surface of the alcohol/water mixture in the glass. Ask this student to carefully tip over the spoon. A single glob of oil should slide into the glass. **It is very important that the oil flow in one continuous stream into the glass, or you will have multiple globs of oil.** You may want to demonstrate the process prior to students trying the procedure.

3. A perfectly spherical glob of oil should be floating in the middle of the glass containing the alcohol/water mixture. Tell students that the forces holding the glob of oil together are just like the forces that hold an atom together.

4. Ask students to select one student in the group to use the cream cheese spreader to force the glob of oil apart. Tell students that this student and the cream cheese spreader will act as a neutron does when an atom is split. The glob of oil will resist this motion. Tell students that they may observe this resistance when they see the glob of oil begin to bulge.

5. Have the student using the cream cheese spreader pass it to another student to try to separate the glob of oil. Students may continue passing the cream cheese spreader until enough force has been exerted that the glob of oil separates into two round drops of oil.

6. Ask students to put their materials down once the glob has separated into two drops of oil. Tell students that atoms behave in the same way that the oil did. Ask students what it took to split the atom. (*A sufficient amount of force was necessary for the atom to split.*)

7. Distribute **Systems Diagram** (Handout 7.1) to students. Ask them to use the diagram to depict what happens when an atom splits. Suggested answers have been provided for teacher's use. The **Systems Diagram** (Handout 7.1) should be stapled or glued into **Problem Logs** for future reference.

Problem Log

- Distribute **Problem Log Questions** (Handout 7.2) and assign for class work or homework.

Assessment

- Use responses to **Problem Log Questions** to determine to what degree students can explain the atom as a system and can generate appropriate questions about nuclear power.

Name _____   Date _____

Systems Diagram

Name of System _____

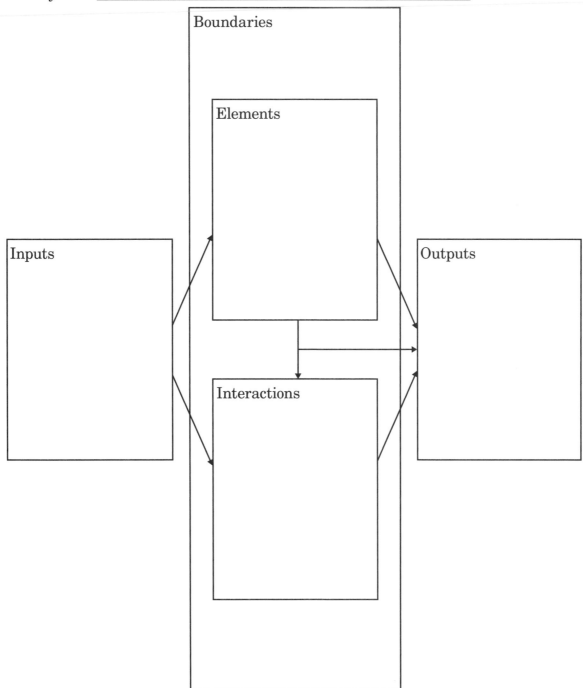

Systems Diagram: Suggested Responses
(Teacher Resource 1)

Name of System: Nuclear Fission of an Atom

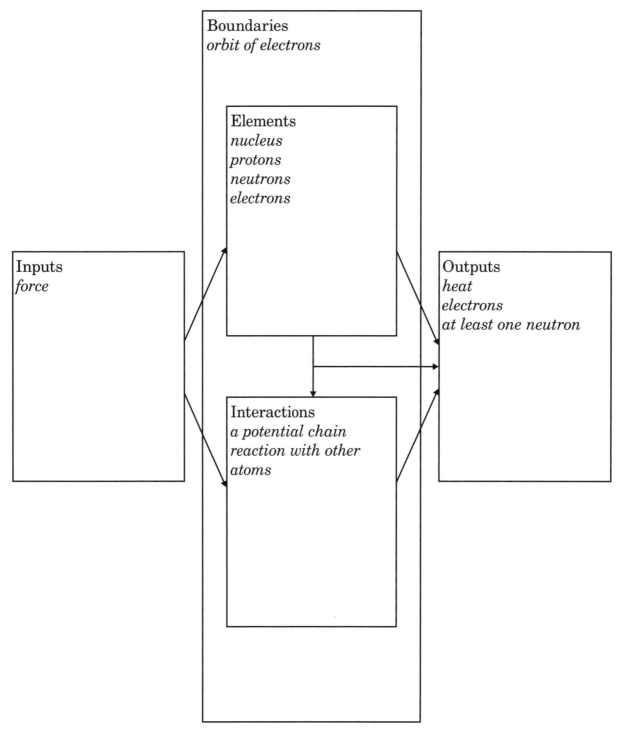

Name _____   Date _____

Problem Log Questions

1. How is an atom like a system?

2. Do you have additional questions about nuclear power generation that need to be answered? List those questions in the space provided.

Radioactive Decay and Half-Life

8

Instructional Purpose

- To develop a physical understanding of half-life through an activity
- To develop a conceptual understanding of half-life as it pertains to radioactive materials

Curriculum Alignment

 Goal 1
Concept

 Goal 2
Content

 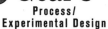 Goal 3
Process/
Experimental Design

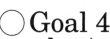 Goal 4
Process/
Reasoning

 ## Vocabulary

Half-Life The rate of decrease of a radioactive element; the amount of time it takes for half of the atoms in a quantity of a radioisotope to decay

Isotope One or more atoms having the same atomic number but a different mass number; this is because they have equal numbers of protons but differing numbers of neutrons

Radioactive Decay The process by which radioactive materials become less radioactive over time

Materials/Resources

Note: The quantity of the first four items listed here is *per group*.

- One shoe box
- 200 or more pennies per group

- 200 or more brass paper fasteners per group
- 200 or more six-sided dice per group
- Three sheets of graph paper per student (Optional: Graphing could be performed by using a computerized graphing program.)
- Student Brainstorming Guide (Handout 8.1)
- Experimental Design Planner (Handout 8.2)
- Experimental Protocol (Handout 8.3)
- Sample Experimental Protocol (Teacher Resource 1)
- Data Tables (Handout 8.4)
- Laboratory Report (Handout 8.5)
- Sample Problem Log Questions (Handout 8.6)

- Problem Log Questions (Handout 8.7)
- Discussion Questions (Handout 8.8)
- Decay Products of Radioisotopes (Handout 8.9)
- Challenge Questions (Handout 8.10)

Lesson Length

Three 60-minute sessions: one each for planning, activities, and discussion

 Sessions 1 and 2 Activities

1. Review the **Need to Know Board** and discuss why half-life would be an important concept to understand and explain at the town meeting. Emphasize that half-life is an important consideration in the safe handling of any radioactive substance.

2. Talk about ways to test half-life of radioactive materials. Discuss half-life in terms other than radioactive materials.

3. Many things grow at a fairly steady rate: population, money in the bank, and the thickness of paper that is continuously folded over onto itself. Many other things decrease at a steady rate: the value of money in the bank, the amount of vacant area in a place where population is growing, and the amount of material undergoing radioactive decay. Radioactive materials become less radioactive over time as a result of a process known as radioactive decay. An understanding of radioactive decay is essential to an understanding of the plans for permanent disposal of radioactive wastes. A useful way to describe the rate of decrease is in terms of *half-life:* the rate of decrease of a radioactive element; the amount of time it takes for half of the atoms in a quantity of a radioisotope to decay. For steady decrease, called exponential decay, the half-life always stays the same. Radioactive materials are characterized by their rates of decay and are rated in terms of their half-lives.

4. Show students the materials for the lesson. Tell the students that they will be using these materials to simulate half-life. They may use the following rules for "decay" of each of the materials:
   - pennies: eliminate all that land heads up
   - brass fasteners: eliminate the ones that land on their heads
   - dice: eliminate those that land with the one's side up

5. Divide students into small groups and ask them to develop a method for measuring the half-life of various substances using the materials available. Distribute copies of the **Student Brainstorming Guide** (Handout 8.1) and have them complete it. To prompt student brainstorming, refer to the questions in the "Ask" section that follows.

6. Discuss the brainstorming results as a class.

7. Distribute copies of the **Experimental Design Planner** (Handout 8.2). Have the class complete it together and review the meaning of each of the terms.

8. After they have completed the **Experimental Design Planners** (Handout 8.2), have each group write their experiment protocol on the **Experimental Protocol** (Handout 8.3). See the **Sample Experimental Protocol** (Teacher Resource 1) as an example of the experimental procedure students might develop. They should include every step they plan to take, the materials they will use, and a data table to record their data. Students should also indicate what safety procedures they plan to use as a part of the overall experimental design.

9. Have students come together as a class and reach a consensus on an experiment protocol.

10. The class should be separated into groups of two to four students depending upon the availability of materials for each group. If the availability of materials is problematic, have the groups share the materials by setting up work stations: one with a shoe box and pennies, another with a shoe box and dice, and a third with a shoe box and brass fasteners.

11. After students perform their experiments, have them complete the **Laboratory Report** (Handout 8.5). Bring the group together to discuss their results, limitations of the results, and possible revisions in experimental design.

12. Have students complete **Sample Problem Log Questions** (Handout 8.6).

    Note: The questions in **Sample Problem Log Questions** (Handout 8.6) reflect the use of the sample **Experimental Protocol** (Handout 8.3). This handout should be modified to reflect the experimental protocol developed by the students. Students may record answers on **Data Tables** (Handout 8.4). If you try the experiment in advance, the range of answers for **Sample Problem Log Questions** (Handout 8.6) will be readily apparent.

13. Discuss answers to questions 1 through 5 on **Sample Problem Log Questions** (Handout 8.6). Then have students complete **Problem Log Questions** (Handout 8.7).

14. **Ask:**
    • What do you think half-life is in terms of radioactive materials?
    • How could we demonstrate half-life with these materials?
    • Will the half-lives be different for the different materials?
    • What characteristics about the materials will determine their individual half-lives?

 Assessment

• Use responses to **Problem Log Questions** to determine student understanding of the concepts of radioactive decay and half-life.

• Evaluate the **Experimental Protocol** for student understanding of experimental design.

Session 3 Note

- This lesson will clarify that radioactive materials lose their radioactivity over time through the process of radioactive decay. Additionally, students will learn that the time for radioactive materials to lose essentially all their radioactivity can vary from seconds to thousands of years. The half-life of a radioisotope is the time it takes for a quantity of it to lose half of its present radioactivity. The necessity of providing safe disposal of radioactive wastes will be discussed.

 ## Session 3 Activities

1. Discuss the students' answers to Question 6 of the half-life activity in **Sample Problem Log Questions** (Handout 8.6). Compare and contrast the usefulness of knowing the half-life of pennies, dice, and/or brass fasteners to the usefulness of knowing the half-life of radioactive waste.

2. Divide the class into small groups and distribute **Discussion Questions** (Handout 8.8). Students should complete the chart collaboratively and answer the discussion questions.

3. Bring the students back into the large group to share answers.

4. Again, divide the class into small groups and distribute **Decay Products of Radioisotopes** (Handout 8.9). Have the students collaboratively answer and discuss the related questions.

5. Bring the students back together into the large group and discuss each group's conclusions.

6. **Ask:**
   - Describe the similarities and differences between the half-life activity from the previous session and the half-life of radioactive substances.
   - Do you think it would be possible to predict when a radioisotope will decay and produce radiation? Why or why not?
   - After a radioisotope decays, is it necessarily stable and nonradioactive?
   - Discuss the meaning of the term *decay chain*.
   - What are the implications for proper waste disposal for radioisotopes that do not decay into stable substances?
   - What do you think is the relationship, if any, between the intensity of the radioactivity of a radioisotope and its half-life?

 ## Extending Student Learning

- Use **Challenge Questions** (Handout 8.10) for extension purposes.

Assessment

- Use responses to **Discussion Questions** to determine student understanding of the concepts of radioactive decay and half-life.
- Evaluate the **Challenge Questions** for student understanding of the concepts of radioactive decay and half-life.

Technology Integration

- Graphing could be performed by using a computerized graphing program.
- Students may use the Internet to explore additional concepts related to nuclear energy production and nuclear waste.
- Encourage students to visit the website of the U.S. Environmental Protection Agency (http://www.epa.gov/radiation/students) to learn more about radiation and its impact on humans.

Name _____   Date _____

Student Brainstorming Guide

1. What do we need to find out? (What is the scientific problem?)

2. What materials do we have available?

continued

Copyright © Kendall/Hunt Publishing Company

3. How can we use these materials to help us find out?

4. What do we think will happen? (What is our hypothesis?)

5. What will we need to observe or measure in order to find out the answer to our scientific question?

Name _____   Date _____

Experimental Design Planner

Title:

_____

Hypothesis (educated guess about what will happen):

_____

Independent variable (the variable that you change):

_____

Dependent variable (the variable that responds to changes in the independent variable):

_____

Observations/Measurements:

_____

Constants (all the things or factors that remain the same):

_____

Control (the standard for comparing experimental effects):

Name   Date

Experimental Protocol

1. List the materials you will need.

2. Write a step-by-step description of what you will do (like a recipe!). List every action you will take during the experiment.

3. What data will you be collecting?

4. Design a data table to collect and analyze your information.

Sample Experimental Protocol
(Teacher Resource 1)

Procedure

If it is not possible to obtain enough materials for each group, arrange the materials in stations around the room. Station 1 will have a shoe box and pennies; Station 2 will have a shoe box and dice; and Station 3 will have a shoe box and brass fasteners. Allow each group to take turns collecting data from each station.

1. Place the pennies in a shoe box, and place the lid on the box. Shake the box for several seconds. Open the box and remove all the pennies that are heads up. Count these, and record the number in **Data Table A** (see Handout 8.4 as an example). Do not put the removed pennies back in the box.

2. Repeat Step 1 over and over until one or no pennies remain in the box. Record the number of pennies removed during each trial in **Data Table A.**

3. Calculate the number of pennies remaining after each shake by subtracting the number of pennies removed each time from the previous number remaining, and record in **Data Table A.**

4. Graph the number of pennies remaining after each shake (vertical axis) versus the number of shakes (horizontal axis). Draw a smooth line that best fits the points.

5. Repeat steps 1 to 5, but substitute the six-sided dice for the pennies. After each thorough shake, remove dice with the one's side up. Record information on **Data Table B.**

6. Repeat steps 1 to 5, but substitute the brass fasteners for the pennies. After each thorough shake, dump the brass fasteners out of the box onto the table. Remove all the brass fasteners that stand on their heads, as you did for the pennies that were heads up. Place the remainder of the brass fasteners back into the box and continue as stated earlier. Record information on **Data Table C.**

Data Tables

Data Table A: Pennies

Total Number of Pennies =

Shake Number	Number of Pennies Removed	Number of Pennies Remaining	Shake Number	Number of Pennies Removed	Number of Pennies Remaining
1			9		
2			10		
3			11		
4			12		
5			13		
6			14		
7			15		
8			16		

Data Table B: Dice

Total Number of Dice =

Shake Number	Number of Dice Removed	Number of Dice Remaining	Shake Number	Number of Dice Removed	Number of Dice Remaining
1			11		
2			12		
3			13		
4			14		
5			15		
6			16		
7			17		
8			18		
9			19		
10			20		

continued

Data Table C: Brass Fasteners

Total Number of Brass Fasteners =

Shake Number	Number of Fasteners Removed	Number of Fasteners Remaining	Shake Number	Number of Fasteners Removed	Number of Fasteners Remaining
1			13		
2			14		
3			15		
4			16		
5			17		
6			18		
7			19		
8			20		
9			21		
10			22		
11			23		
12			24		

Laboratory Report

1. What did you do or test? (Include your experiment title.)

2. How did you do it? Cite materials and methods. You can go back to your
   Experimental Protocol (Handout 8.3) and use the information from the
   first two questions.

3. What did you find out? (Include a data summary and the explanation of its
   meaning.)

continued

4. What did you learn from your experiment?

5. What additional questions do you now have?

6. Does the information you learned help with the problem?

Sample Problem Log Questions

This is based on the **Sample Experimental Protocol.**

1. What does each graph represent?

2. Approximately what percentage of the remaining pennies, dice, and brass fasteners was remaining after each shake? Why?

continued

3. Determine the half-life of:

   a. The pennies assuming one shake represents 4 years.

   b. The dice assuming one shake represents 15 minutes.

   c. The brass fasteners assuming one shake represents 0.75 seconds.

Copyright © Kendall/Hunt Publishing Company

continued

4. Using the half-lives determined in Question 3, calculate:

   a. The age of the penny shoe box when only ten pennies remain.

   b. The age of the die shoe box when only fifty dice remain.

   c. The age of the brass fastener shoe box when only seventy-five remain.

continued

5. Using the half-lives determined in question 3, what percentage of the total number of pennies used in this experiment would be left after 9 years? Percentage of dice left after 25 minutes? Percentage of brass fasteners left after 0.15 seconds?

6. Compare and contrast the usefulness of knowing the half-life of pennies, dice, and/or brass fasteners to the usefulness of knowing the half-life of radioactive waste.

Name _____   Date _____

Problem Log Questions

Referring to our **Need to Know Board,** where could half-life fit in the problem? Why is knowing how to calculate half-life important to an understanding of nuclear power?

Name _____   Date _____

Discussion Questions

Radioisotope	Type of Decay	Half-Life	How long it will take to lose		
			3/4 of Its Radioactivity	7/8 of Its Radioactivity	1/10 of Its Radioactivity
Natural Elements					
Uranium-235	Alpha	7.10×10^8 yr			
Uranium-238	Alpha			1.35×10^{10} yr	
Transuranics					
Plutonium-238	Alpha		172 yr		
Plutonium-239	Alpha	24,400 yr			
Plutonium-240	Alpha			19,740 yr	
Plutonium-241	Beta		26.4 yr		
Americium-241	Alpha	458 yr			
Americium-243	Alpha				1,474 yr
Neptunium-239	Beta		4.7 yr		
Fission Products					
Cerium-144	Beta			2.40 yr	
Cesium-137	Beta		66.4 yr		
Iodine-131	Beta				38.74 hr
Krypton-85	Beta	10.72 yr			
Molybdenum-99	Beta		133.4 hr		
Strontium-90	Beta	28.1 yr			
Xenon-133	Beta		10.54 days		
Other Radioactive Materials					
Praseodymium-144	Beta	17.3 min			
Barium-137	Alpha		3.04 min		
Thorium-231	Beta				5.1 hr
Thorium-234	Beta		48.2 days		
Uranium-234	Alpha	247,000 yr			
Americium-241	Alpha			1,374 yr	
Neptunium-237	Alpha				4.28×10^5 yr
Neptunium-239	Beta	2.35 days			
Technetium-99	Gamma		12 hr		
Yttrium-90	Alpha	64 hr			

continued

1. What is the general relationship between the intensity of radioactivity and half-life? Explain your answer.

2. In your own words, explain the significance of the preceding information as it relates to disposing of radioactive waste permanently.

Name _____ Date _____

Decay Products of Radioisotopes

Radioisotope	Type of Decay	Half-Life	Radioactive Decay Products		
			Product of Decay	Type of Decay	Half-Life
Natural Elements					
Uranium-235	Alpha	7.10×10^8 yr	Thorium-231	Beta	25.5 hr
Uranium-238	Alpha	4.5×10^9 yr	Thorium-234	Beta	24.1 days
Transuranics					
Plutonium-238	Alpha	86 yr	Uranium-234	Alpha	247,000 yr
Plutonium-239	Alpha	24,400 yr	Uranium-235	Alpha	7.10×10^8 yr
Plutonium-240	Alpha	6.580 yr	Uranium-236	Alpha	2.39×10^7 yr
Plutonium-241	Beta	13.2 yr	Americium-241	Alpha	458 yr
Americium-241	Alpha	458 yr	Neptunium-237	Alpha	2.14×10^6 yr
Americium-243	Alpha	7,370 yr	Neptunium-239	Beta	2.35 days
Neptunium-239	Beta	2.35 days	Plutonium-239	Alpha	24,400 yr
Fission Products					
Cerium-144	Beta	285 days	Praseodymium-144	Beta	17.3 min
Cesium-137	Beta	30.2 yr	Barium-137	Alpha	1.52 min
Iodine-131	Beta	8.07 days	Xenon-131	Stable	
Krypton-85	Beta	10.72 yr	Redidium-85	Stable	
Molybdenum-99	Beta	66.7 hr	Technetrium-99	Gamma	6 hr
Strontium-90	Beta	28.1 yr	Yttrium-90	Alpha	64 hr
Xenon-133	Beta	5.27 days	Cesium-133	Stable	

continued

1. Discuss the implications the information contained in the chart on the previous page has on nuclear waste disposal, particularly the fission products.

2. What do you think is meant by the term "decay chain"?

3. Identify the longest decay chain possible on this handout. Why is it the longest?

Name _____   Date _____

Challenge Questions

1. What percentage of the original radioactivity of a quantity of a radioisotope remains after each half-life?

   1   2   3   4   5   6   7   8   9   10

   __   __   __   __   __   __   __   __   __   __

2. Using a piece of graph paper, plot the decay curve from the data in Question 1. Try to draw a smooth curved line connecting each point. (Half-life should be on the horizontal axis, while percentage should be on the vertical axis.)

3. Using the graph from Question 2:
   a. What percentage of the quantity will be left after 2 ½ half-lives?

   b. How many half-lives does it take to be left with only 10 percent of the original radioisotope?

   c. If each half-life represents 75 seconds, how long would it take to reduce the radioactivity of the original radioisotope to 5 percent of its original value?

continued

4. Radium has a half-life of 1,600 years. Approximately how long does it take for 1 percent of a sample of radium to decay?

5. Xenon-133 has a half-life of 5.27 days. Approximately how long does it take for 17 percent of a sample of radium to decay?

6. Scientists believe the earth is 4.6 billion years old. Calculate what percentage of the Uranium-238 originally present is here now if the half-life of Uranium-238 is 4.5 billion years.

continued

7. A certain amount of Uranium-235 remains in the fuel rods of a nuclear reactor after it is used to produce power. The leftover Uranium-235 is part of the waste that now needs to be disposed of permanently. If originally only 1 ounce of Uranium-235 is left over, how long would it take for 0.00005 ounce of lead-207 to be produced through the following decay chain?

	Half-life
U-235	7.10×10^8 years
Th-231	25.5 hours
Pa-231	27 days
Ac-227	10 days
Fr-223	4.8 minutes
Ra-223	1,600 years
Rn-219	3.8 days
Po-215	4.2×10^6 seconds
Pb-211	3.3 hours
Bi-211	47 minutes
Tl-207	2.20 minutes
Pb-207	Stable

Safety and Radiation Effects on People

9

Instructional Purpose

• To introduce the safety issues related to nuclear power

Curriculum Alignment

 Goal 1
Concept

 Goal 2
Content

 Goal 3
Process/
Experimental Design

○ Goal 4
Process/
Reasoning

 Vocabulary

Nuclear Radiation Ionizing radiation (alpha, beta, and gamma) originating in the nuclei of radioactive atoms

Nuclear Waste Radioactive by-products from any activity, including energy production, weapons production, and medical treatment and research

Nucleus The central part of an atom that contains the protons and neutrons

Proton A subatomic particle in the nucleus of an atom with about the same mass as the neutron but carrying a positive charge

Radiation Energy emitted in the form of rays or particles that are potentially harmful to humans; it moves through space in the form of particles or electromagnetic waves

Radioactive A property of some materials whereby spontaneous emissions of alpha or beta particles or gamma rays occur; these particles and rays are potentially harmful to humans.

 Materials/Resources

• Need to Know Board
• Emergency Preparedness at Nuclear Power Plants (Handout 9.1)
• "How Safe Is Safe Enough?" Discussion Questions (Handout 9.2)
• Student Brainstorming Guide (Handout 9.3)

- Experimental Design Planner (Handout 9.4)
- Experimental Protocol (Handout 9.5)

Lesson Length

Two 60-minute sessions

 ## Session 1 Activities

1. Discuss the **Need to Know Board** in terms of safe operation of the power plant and radiation safety for people.
2. Have students read **Emergency Preparedness at Nuclear Power Plants** (Handout 9.1).
3. Divide the class into small groups and have them discuss their thoughts about this information. Have them respond to **How Safe Is Safe Enough? Discussion Questions** (Handout 9.2).
4. **Ask:**
   - What role does safety play in our problem?
   - Do you think it is necessary to look at safety before making a decision? Why or why not?
   - How will this help us conceptualize safety in a nuclear plant?

 ## Extending Student Learning

Wolfson, R. (1993). *Nuclear choices: A citizen's guide to nuclear technology.* Cambridge, MA: The MIT Press. (ISBN 0-262-73108-8)

This book is strongly recommended as an additional reading source, particularly for this lesson, but also for the unit as a whole.

 ## Assessment

- Evaluate student participation in the class discussion for understanding of the safety issues related to nuclear power.

Name   Date

Emergency Preparedness at Nuclear Power Plants

Background

The Nuclear Regulatory Commission (NRC) reexamined the role of emergency preparedness (EP) for protecting the public near nuclear power plants following the accident at the Three Mile Island nuclear power plant in 1979. The accident showed the need for improved planning, response, and communication by federal, state, and local governments to deal with reactor accidents. Although the NRC remained vigilant over the years, the events of September 11, 2001, prompted a new focus on emergency preparedness and a further review of the threat environment. The NRC now considers new threat scenarios and protections in emergency preparedness in light of the threat of terrorist attacks.

Nuclear power plant owners, government agencies, state and local officials, as well as thousands of volunteers and first responders have worked together for more than 20 years to create a system of emergency preparedness and response that will serve the public well in the unlikely event of an emergency. The nuclear power plants' emergency plans include preparations for evacuation, sheltering, or other actions to protect the residents near nuclear power plants in the event of a serious incident.

Since commercial nuclear power plants began operating in the United States, there have been no physical injuries or fatalities from exposure to radiation from the plants among members of the U.S. public. Even the country's worst nuclear power plant accident at Three Mile Island resulted in no identifiable health impacts.

Federal Oversight

In the U.S., 104 commercial nuclear power reactors are licensed to operate at 65 sites in 31 states. For each site, there are onsite and offsite emergency plans to assure that adequate protective measures can be taken to protect the public in the event of a radiological emergency. Federal oversight of emergency preparedness for licensed nuclear power plants is shared by the NRC and Federal Emergency Management Agency (FEMA). This sharing is facilitated through a Memorandum of Understanding (MOU).

The MOU is responsive to the President's decision of December 7, 1979, that FEMA take the lead in overseeing offsite planning and response, and that NRC assist FEMA in carrying out this role. The NRC has

Source: United States Nuclear Regulatory Commission, Office of Public Affairs, Washington, DC 20555, Telephone: 301-415-8200; E-mail: opa@nrc.gov; http://adamswebsearch2.nrc.gov/idmws/ doccontent.dll?library=PU_ADAMS^PBNTAD01&ID=062500133:16

continued

statutory responsibility for the radiological health and safety of the public by overseeing onsite preparedness and has overall authority for both onsite and offsite emergency preparedness.

Before a plant is licensed to operate, the NRC must have "reasonable assurance that adequate protective measures can and will be taken in the event of a radiological emergency." The NRC's decision of reasonable assurance is based on licensees complying with NRC regulations and guidance. In addition, licensees and area response organizations must demonstrate they can effectively implement emergency plans and procedures during periodic evaluated exercises. As part of the Reactor Oversight Process, the NRC reviews licensees' emergency planning procedures and training. These reviews include regular drills and exercises that assist licensees in identifying areas for improvement, such as in the interface of security operations and emergency preparedness. Each plant owner is required to exercise its emergency plan with the NRC, FEMA, and offsite authorities at least once every two years to ensure state and local officials remain proficient in implementing their emergency plans. Licensees also self-test their emergency plans regularly by conducting drills. Each plant's performance in drills and exercises can be accessed through the NRC website at this address: http://www.nrc.gov/NRR/OVERSIGHT/ASSESS/index.html.

FEMA takes the lead in initially reviewing and assessing the offsite planning and response and in assisting state and local governments, while the NRC reviews and assesses the onsite planning and response. FEMA findings and determinations as to the adequacy and capability of implementing offsite plans are communicated to the NRC. The NRC reviews the FEMA findings and determinations as well as the onsite findings. The NRC then makes a determination on the overall state of emergency preparedness. These overall findings and determinations are used by the NRC to make radiological health and safety decisions before issuing licenses and in the continuing oversight of operating reactors. The NRC has the authority to take action, including shutting down any reactor deemed not to provide reasonable assurance of the protection of public health and safety.

Emergency Planning Zones

For planning purposes, the NRC defines two emergency planning zones (EPZs) around each nuclear power plant. The exact size and configuration of the zones vary from plant to plant due to local emergency response needs and capabilities, population, land characteristics, access routes, and jurisdictional boundaries. The two types of EPZs are: The plume exposure pathway EPZ extends about 10 miles in radius around a plant. Its primary concern is the exposure of the public to, and the inhalation of,

continued

airborne radioactive contamination. The ingestion pathway EPZ extends about 50 miles in radius around a plant. Its primary concern is the ingestion of food and liquid that is contaminated by radioactivity.

Emergency Classification

Emergency Classification is a set of plant conditions which indicate a level of risk to the public. Nuclear power plants use the four emergency classifications listed below in order of increasing severity.

Notification of Unusual Event—Under this category, events are in process or have occurred which indicate potential degradation in the level of safety of the plant. No release of radioactive material requiring offsite response or monitoring is expected unless further degradation occurs.

Alert—If an alert is declared, events are in process or have occurred that involve an actual or potential substantial degradation in the level of safety of the plant. Any releases of radioactive material from the plant are expected to be limited to a small fraction of the Environmental Protection Agency (EPA) protective action guides (PAGs). Additional information regarding PAGs can be found on the EPA Web site at: http://www.epa.gov/radiation/rert/pags.htm.

Site Area Emergency—A site area emergency involves events in process or which have occurred that result in actual or likely major failures of plant functions needed for protection of the public. Any releases of radioactive material are not expected to exceed the EPA PAGs except near the site boundary.

General Emergency—A general emergency involves actual or imminent substantial core damage or melting of reactor fuel with the potential for loss of containment integrity. Radioactive releases during a general emergency can reasonably be expected to exceed the EPA PAGs for more than the immediate site area.

Protective Actions

The NRC's regulations are designed to mitigate accident consequences and minimize radiation exposure to the public through protective actions. When a radiological emergency occurs, nuclear power plant personnel evaluate plant conditions and make protective action recommendations to the state and local government agencies on how to protect the population. Based on the recommendation and independent assessment of other local factors, the state or local government agencies are responsible for making

continued

decisions on the actions necessary to protect the public and for relaying these decisions to the public.

Factors that affect protective action decisions include plant conditions, competing events, weather, evacuation times, shelter factors, how quickly an incident develops, how short-lived a release of radiation may be, and other conditions.

Evacuation, Sheltering, and the Use of Potassium Iodide

Protective actions considered for a radiological emergency include evacuation, sheltering, and, as a supplement to these, the prophylactic use of potassium iodide (KI), as appropriate. Under most conditions, evacuation may be preferred to remove the public from further exposure to radioactive material. However, under some conditions, people may be instructed to take shelter in their homes, schools, or office buildings. Depending on the type of structure, sheltering can significantly reduce a person's dose compared to remaining outside. In certain situations, KI is used as a supplement to sheltering.

Evacuation does not always call for completely emptying the 10-mile zone around a nuclear power plant. In most cases, the release of radioactive material from a plant during a major incident would move with the wind, not in all directions surrounding the plant. The release would also expand and become less concentrated as it travels away from a plant. Therefore, evacuations should be mapped to anticipate the path of the release. Generally as a minimum, in the event of a General Emergency, a two-mile ring around the plant is evacuated, along with people living in the 5-mile zone directly downwind and slightly to either side of the projected path of the release. This "keyhole" pattern helps account for potential wind shifts and fluctuations in the release path. Evacuation beyond 5 miles is assessed as the accident progresses. Also in response to a General Emergency, people living in the remainder of the 10-mile zone will most likely be advised to go indoors to monitor Emergency Alert System broadcasts.

Sheltering is a protective action that keeps people indoors, such as at home, the office, school, or a shopping mall to reduce exposure to radioactive material. It may be appropriate to shelter when the release of radioactive material is known to be short-term or controlled by the nuclear power plant operator. Additional information on evacuation and sheltering can be found on the NRC Web site at http://www.nrc.gov/what-we-do/emerg-preparedness/evacuation-sheltering.html.

Another protective action in the 10-mile EPZ involves KI, a compound that helps prevent the thyroid from absorbing radioactive iodine, one of several radioactive materials that could be present in a release from a nuclear power plant accident. If taken within the appropriate time and at the appropriate dosage, KI blocks the radioactive iodine from being absorbed by the thyroid gland and reduces the risk of thyroid

continued

cancers and other diseases. KI does not protect against any other inhaled radioactive materials, nor will it offer protection from external exposure to radiation. The Food and Drug Administration (FDA) has determined that KI is a safe and effective drug when used for this purpose. However, there may be risks and potential side effects in using KI, including gastrointestinal disturbances, allergic reactions, and iodide goiter and hypothyroidism. Please consult your physician if you have questions on the potential side effects.

In January 2001, the NRC modified its regulations to include considering the use of KI, and, later that year, the FDA issued guidance on using the drug. As of February 28, 2005, 20 states have received KI tablets from the NRC for their populations within 10 miles of a nuclear power plant. These states are: Alabama, Arizona, California, Connecticut, Delaware, Florida, Maryland, Massachusetts, Mississippi, New Hampshire, New Jersey, New York, North Carolina, Ohio, Pennsylvania, South Carolina, Tennessee, Vermont, Virginia, and West Virginia. Illinois has its own KI program in place; therefore, 21 of the 34 states with populations within the 10-mile EPZ have KI. Further information on KI is available on the NRC Web site at: http://www.nrc.gov/what-we-do/emerg-preparedness/protect-public/potassium-iodide-use.html.

Terrorism and Emergency Preparedness

After September 2001, the NRC examined how terrorist-based events might challenge existing emergency preparedness. The NRC's formal evaluation determined that, in view of the threat environment, the emergency preparedness planning basis remain valid. While a terrorist event might alter the initial response to an event, the consequences of the event will be the same whether it was caused by terrorism or a safety accident. The nuclear power reactor's emergency plans are periodically updated and are designed to be flexible to identify, evaluate and react to the wide spectrum of emergency conditions. The NRC recognized how the terrorism threat affects emergency planning when it issued orders and guidance to nuclear power plants after September 2001. These orders and guidance included interim measures dealing with how increased security affects implementation of emergency plans. Nuclear industry groups and federal, state, and local government agencies assisted in the prompt implementation of these measures and participated in drills and exercises to test these new planning elements. The NRC has reviewed licensees' commitments to address these requirements and verified the implementation through inspections to ensure public health and safety.

"How Safe Is Safe Enough?" Discussion Questions

1. Why is "absolute protection, total absence of risk" neither a possible nor meaningful goal for nuclear plants? Why is it impossible to achieve?

2. What other aspects of everyday life offer as much, or more, risk to people than a nuclear power plant? Why?

3. What precautions would make you feel safe living in a neighborhood with a nuclear power facility? Why?

Name _____   Date _____

Student Brainstorming Guide

1. What do we need to find out? (What is the scientific problem?)

2. What materials do we have available?

Source: Cothron, J. G., Giese, R. N. & Rezba, R. J. (1989). *Students and research.* Dubuque, IA: Kendall/Hunt Publishing

continued

3. How can we use these materials to help us find out?

4. What do we think will happen? (What is our hypothesis?)

5. What will we need to observe or measure in order to find out the answer to our scientific question?

Name _____   Date _____

Experimental Design Planner

Title:

_____

Hypothesis (educated guess about what will happen):

_____

Independent variable (the variable that you change):

_____

Dependent variable (the variable that responds to changes in the independent variable):

_____

Observations/Measurements:

_____

Constants (all the things or factors that remain the same):

_____

Control (the standard for comparing experimental effects):

Name   Date

Experimental Protocol

1. List the materials you will need.

2. Write a step-by-step description of what you will do (like a recipe!). List every action you will take during the experiment.

continued

3. What data will you be collecting?

4. Design a data table to collect and analyze your information.

Radiation Exposure

10

Instructional Purpose

- To understand that radiation is a natural part of the environment and affects students' lives daily

---

Curriculum Alignment   ◯ Goal 1 *Concept*   ● Goal 2 *Content*   ● Goal 3 *Process/ Experimental Design*   ◯ Goal 4 *Process/ Reasoning*

Vocabulary

Alpha Particles The most energetic of the three types of radiation; alpha particles lose their energy almost as soon as they come into contact with an object

Beta Particles Smaller than alpha particles, beta particles can pass through paper but may be stopped by glass such as that found in windows.

Gamma Rays Waves of electromagnetic energy that is very penetrating and is best shielded by lead

Isotope One or more atoms having the same atomic number but a different mass number; this is because they have equal numbers of protons but differing numbers of neutrons.

Millirem Unit of measure of radiation; this is one-thousandth (10^{-3}) of a rem

Radioactive A property of some materials whereby spontaneous emissions of alpha or beta particles or gamma rays occur; these particles and rays are potentially harmful to humans.

Radiation Energy emitted in the form of rays or particles that are potentially harmful to humans

Materials/Resources

- Personal Annual Radiation Dose (Handout 10.1)

Lesson Length

60 minutes

 **Activities**

1. Ask students if they cited waste as a potential problem when they have been considering the problem situation. Discuss waste as a concern of all industries and ask students to give examples from industries other than nuclear power plants.

2. Explain to students that radiation is all around us as it is a natural part of the environment. Tell students that radiation is measured in *millirems* (mrem).

3. Distribute **Personal Annual Radiation Dose** (Handout 10.1) and review with students. Explain that the average person's annual mrem dose is 350 mrem, so students' personal annual totals should not meet or exceed 350 mrem!

4. Read through **Personal Annual Radiation Dose** (Handout 10.1) with students to make sure they understand what they are being asked to do. Explain that they should only provide answers to the medical questions if they have had the procedure within the past year.

5. Have students complete **Personal Annual Radiation Dose** (Handout 10.1) independently. Explain to students that they may ask a group member for assistance if needed as they work through the sheet.

6. After students have completed **Personal Annual Radiation Dose** (Handout 10.1), lead a class discussion about student responses. **Ask:**

   • Were you surprised at the dose of radiation you receive annually? Why or why not?

   • What has the awareness of your personal annual radiation dose inspired you to do or learn about radiation?

   • When considering your role with the Nuclear Regulatory Commission, what kinds of issues will you have to handle with stakeholders when they learn that you want to expand an already potentially dangerous industry and possibly increase their annual doses of radiation?

Note

• The amount of radiation exposure is usually expressed in a unit called millirem (mrem). In the United States, the average person is exposed to an effective dose equivalent of approximately 360 mrem (whole-body exposure) per year from all sources (NCRP Report No. 93).

Assessment

- Evaluate student participation in the class discussion.
- Completed **Personal Annual Radiation Dose** (Handout 10.1)

Technology Integration

- As an alternative to completing **Personal Annual Radiation Dose** (Handout 10.1), students can complete a radiation calculation online at http://www.epa.gov/radiation/students/calculate.html.
- Encourage students to visit http://www.epa.gov/radiation/students/people.html to learn about important people in radiation history.

Personal Annual Radiation Dose

1. Radiation from outer space .... <u>26</u>

2. The number of millirems for your elevation (in feet): .... _____

   Up to 1,000 ft = 2   1,000–2,000 ft = 5

   2,000–3,000 ft = 9   3,000–4,000 ft = 9

   4,000–5,000 ft = 21   5,000–6,000 ft = 29

   6,000–7,000 ft = 40   7,000–8,000 ft = 53

   8,000–9,000 ft = 70

3. Radiation from the ground:

   • If you live in a state that borders the Gulf or Atlantic Coast, add 23. .... _____

   • If you live in the Colorado Plateau area (near Denver), add 90. .... _____

   • If you live in middle America (rest of the United States), add 46. .... _____

4. If you live in a stone, brick, or concrete building, add 7. .... _____

   Subtotal for Environment (Add answers 1 through 4.) .... _____

5. Radiation from food and water .... <u>40</u>

6. Radiation from the air (radon) .... <u>200</u>

   Subtotal internal radiation (Add answers 5 through 6.) .... _____

7. Weapons test fallout .... <u>1</u>

8. Jet plane travel (For each 1,000 mi traveled by plane this year, add 1.) .... _____

9. If you have porcelain crowns or false teeth, add 0.07. .... _____

10. If you use gas lantern mantles when camping, add 0.003. .... _____

11. If you use luggage inspection at airports, add 0.002. .... _____

12. If you watch TV, add 1. .... _____

13. If you use a video display terminal, add 1. .... _____

14. If you have a smoke detector, add 0.008. .... _____

Source: Adapted from the U.S. Nuclear Regulatory Commission website at http://www.nrc.gov/reading-rm/basic-ref/teachers/average-dose-worksheet.pdf

continued

15. If you wear a plutonium-powered cardiac pacemaker, add 100.   _____

16. If you have had diagnostic X-rays, add 40.   _____

17. If you have had nuclear medical procedures (e.g. thyroid scan), add 14.   _____

18. If you live within 50 miles of a pressurized water reactor nuclear power plant, add 0.0009   _____

19. If you live within 50 miles of a coal-fired electrical utility plant, add 0.03.   _____

Subtotal Other Sources (Add answers 7 through 19.)   _____

Grand total (Add subtotals from the three categories for a total annual mrems dose.)   _____

Background Radiation

11

Instructional Purpose

- To understand that radiation is a natural part of the environment and affects students' lives daily

Curriculum Alignment

 ○ Goal 1 *Concept*   ● Goal 2 *Content*   ● Goal 3 *Process/ Experimental Design*   ○ Goal 4 *Process/ Reasoning*

 ## Vocabulary

Background Radiation The natural radioactivity in the environment. Background radiation consists of cosmic radiation from outer space, radiation from the radioactive elements in rocks and soil, and radiation from radon and its decay products in the air we breathe.

Nuclear Radiation Ionizing radiation (alpha, beta, and gamma) originating in the nuclei of radioactive atoms

Nuclear Waste Radioactive by-products from any activity, including energy production, weapons production, and medical treatment and research

Radiation Energy emitted in the form of rays or particles that are potentially harmful to humans

Radioactive A property of some materials whereby spontaneous emissions of alpha or beta particles or gamma rays occur; these particles and rays are potentially harmful to humans.

 ## Materials/Resources

- Peanut butter jar
- Dark-colored fabric (black velveteen is best)
- Rubbing alcohol
- Block of dry ice large enough to hold the peanut butter jar
- Corrugated cardboard
- Projector (movie or slide projector) to provide a beam of light
- Plastic tray to hold dry ice
- Resource materials about radiation

- Amateur Scientist column from *Scientific American,* September 1952, p. 179
- Simple Cloud Chamber (Handout 11.1)
- Electromagnetic Spectrum (Teacher Resource 1)
- Problem Log Questions (Handout 11.2)
- Problem Log Questions (Handout 11.3)

Lesson Length

60 minutes

 Activities

1. Discuss radiation with students. Ask them whether or not radiation is a naturally occurring phenomenon or one only generated by artificial means. Through the course of the conversation, probe students for their knowledge about background radiation and its effects. Encourage students to consider the difference between background radiation and other forms of radiation. Ask students why information about background radiation might be important while considering the nuclear power plant problem.

2. Have students consult in-class resources to get answers to some of the basic questions that arise during the discussion.

3. Assemble the cloud chamber as shown in **Simple Cloud Chamber** (Handout 11.1).

4. Block all light from the room. A single projector beam from a movie/slide projector or a strong flashlight should be placed directly to one side of the cloud chamber.

5. Have students watch the chamber and make observations about what they see. Have them discuss the number of times they see a vapor trail inside the cloud chamber. Ask students to speculate about the amount of background radiation they encounter based on this evidence. Use **Electromagnetic Spectrum** (Teacher Resource 1) to show students the wavelengths and frequencies of electromagnetic radiation.

6. If background radiation happens to be low (i.e., no visible trails are produced), place a radioactive source such as a 1930s or 1940s watch with a radium dial in the chamber and repeat. Please follow safety guidelines for handling radioactive materials. There may be too much shielding in your classroom. If so, try taking the cloud chamber outside and putting it inside a large dark box.

7. Students should be provided with resource materials so they can find basic information as questions arise.

8. Have students complete **Problem Log Questions** (Handout 11.2 and Handout 11.3).

9. **Ask:**
   - Is radiation only man-made? What are natural sources of radiation?
   - What man-made sources of radiation are in our daily lives?
   - Why aren't people concerned about background radiation if radiation is so harmful?
   - How could we tell how much radioactive decay is in the room right now?
   - If you could see radioactive decay in the room, what would you be interested in knowing?
   - What do you see in the cloud chamber?
   - What could be producing the radioactive decay in the room?
   - Do the particles you see appear to be different from one another in any way? What differences do you see?
   - What new perspective does this give you on the issue of radioactive decay that comes from nuclear power plants?
   - What additional information do you need about radiation in order to understand the difference (list these on the **Need to Know Board**).

 **Notes**

1. *Background radiation:* Human beings are constantly exposed to naturally occurring background radiation, and any discussion of the risks associated with human use of radioactive materials must also explore the existence and effects of the radiation that we normally experience. There are two principal natural sources of this background radiation: radioactive decay of elements in our surroundings and cosmic rays that originate in space. The sun is a source of many high-energy elementary particles and of high-energy electromagnetic radiation, such as gamma rays, X-rays, and ultraviolet light. When these things enter the atmosphere, some of them are scattered, some hit atoms in the atmosphere and cause the emission of other particles, and some make it all the way to the surface of the earth. The actual levels of background radiation are different at different points on the earth, because the natural abundance of radioactive elements varies and also because the background radiation due to cosmic rays increases with increasing elevation (the less atmosphere that there is to shield against the cosmic rays, the more elements reach the surface).

2. Resources for basic information about cloud chambers and more complex cloud chambers:

Scientific American
December 1956, p. 169
April 1956, p. 156
June 1959, p. 173

3. A lesson plan about cloud chambers allowing students to see the "footprints" of radiation may be found at the Nuclear Regulatory Commission website: http://www.nrc.gov/reading-rm/basic-ref/teachers/unit1.html#activity_1

4. Caution: Dry ice must be handled with care.

   ▪ Dry ice must not be tasted, placed near the mouth, or allowed to touch the skin, as the extremely low temperature could cause a burn.

   ▪ Dry ice must not be placed in glass jars or tightly sealed containers. They could explode due to the high pressure.

   ▪ Do not breathe the gas from dry ice for an extended period in a closed area, such as a car. Store the dry ice in a container such as a styrofoam cooler until you are ready to use it.

   ▪ When the dry ice has served its purpose and you no longer have any use for it, open the container and let the dry ice dissipate in a safe place, preferably outside where students or others will not find it and play with it.

 Extending Student Learning

- *Radon Gas:* Another way that students can explore background radiation is through the use of radon detectors. Radon is a radioactive gas that is produced by the radioactive decay of other elements in rocks or soil. Certain parts of the United States have high concentrations of these elements in their soil; this can result in high concentrations of radon gas in buildings, particularly in areas such as basements. The government has encouraged people to test their homes for radon, as it is thought that long-term exposure to radon can significantly increase a person's risk of lung cancer, particularly if that person also smokes. Radon detectors are relatively cheap and readily available; students could design a testing protocol for their school and/or their homes.

- Have students explore what research has been done to determine whether travel in an airplane exposes one to more radiation than one would be exposed to on the ground.

 **Assessment**

- Evaluate student observations noted in **Problem Logs.**

Simple Cloud Chamber

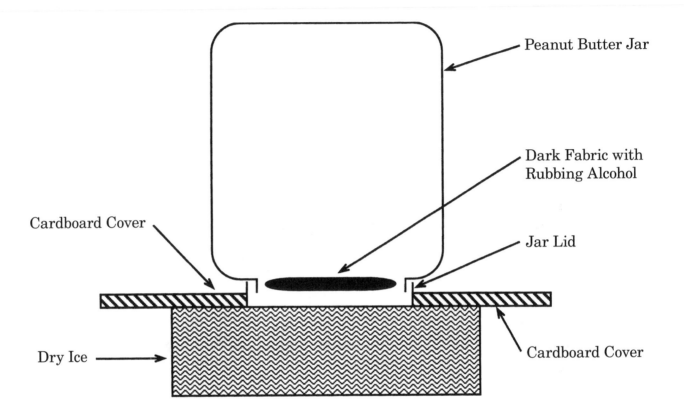

Peanut Butter Jar

Dark Fabric with
Rubbing Alcohol

Cardboard Cover

Jar Lid

Dry Ice

Cardboard Cover

Adapted from: Amateur Scientist Column. (September, 1952). *Scientific American.* p. 179.

Electromagnetic Spectrum
(Teacher Resource 1)

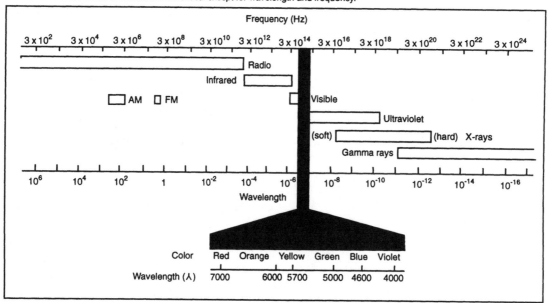

Wavelengths and Frequencies of Electromagnetic Radiation

Type of Radiation	Wavelength Range	Frequency Range
Gamma rays	$< 10^{-4}$	$> 3 \times 10^{19}$ Hz
X rays	$1 - 200 \times 10^{-8}$	$1.5 \times 10^{16} - 3 \times 10^{19}$
Extreme ultraviolet	$200 - 900 \times 10^{-8}$	$3.3 \times 10^{15} - 1.5 \times 10^{16}$
Ultraviolet	$900 - 4000 \times 10^{-8}$	$7.5 \times 10^{14} - 3.3 \times 10^{15}$
Visible	$4000 - 7000 \times 10^{-8}$	$4.3 \times 10^{14} - 7.5 \times 10^{14}$
Near infrared	$0.7 - 20 \times 10^{-4}$	$1.5 \times 10^{13} - 4.3 \times 10^{14}$
Far infrared	$20 - 100 \times 10^{-4}$	$3.0 \times 10^{12} - 1.5 \times 10^{13}$
Radio	> 0.01	$< 3 \times 10^{12}$
(Radar)	$(2 - 20)$	$(1.5 - 15 \times 10^9)$
(FM radio)	$(250 - 350)$	$(85 - 110 \times 10^6)$
(AM radio)	$(18,000 - 55,000)$	$(550 - 1600 \times 10^3)$

*All wavelengths are given in centimeters; recall that 1×10^{-8} cm = 1 Angstrom; and 1×10^{-4} cm = 1 micron (10^{-6} meter)

From T. P. Snow, *Essentials of the Dynamic Universe*, 3rd ed. (Copyright 1970 by West Publishing Company).

Problem Log Questions

Record observations about what you see in the cloud chamber. Observations should include: what the output of the cloud chamber looks like, similarities and differences among the different particles observed, estimate of number of particles observed at any given time; etc.

Name _____ Date _____

Problem Log Questions

We've been discussing systems in this unit: the system of generating nuclear power, the system of a nuclear power plant, the system of nuclear power regulation, and so on. Is the cloud chamber a system? Defend your response.

Shielding Experiment

12

Instructional Purpose

• To introduce experimental design in a relevant context

Curriculum Alignment ○ **Goal 1** Concept ● **Goal 2** Content ● **Goal 3** Process/ Experimental Design ○ **Goal 4** Process/ Reasoning

 Vocabulary

Background Radiation The natural radioactivity in the environment. Background radiation consists of cosmic radiation from outer space, radiation from the radioactive elements in rocks and soil, and radiation from radon and its decay products in the air we breathe.

Nuclear Radiation Ionizing radiation (alpha, beta, and gamma) originating in the nuclei of radioactive atoms

Nuclear Waste Radioactive by-products from any activity, including energy production, weapons production, and medical treatment and research

Radiation Energy emitted in the form of rays or particles that are potentially harmful to humans

Radioactive A property of some materials whereby spontaneous emissions of alpha or beta particles or gamma rays occur; these particles and rays are potentially harmful to humans.

 Materials/Resources

• Ultraviolet light source (e.g., black lightbulb, plant grow lightbulb, or tensor desk lamp bulb)

• Prism

• Ultraviolet light detector (e.g., white cotton T-shirt washed in a detergent that contains brightening agents—All or Tide)

• Shielding materials: cinderblocks, glass, plastic,

177

aluminum, foil (anything that can be tested for its ability to block UV or visible light)

- Plastic UV-protective glasses
- Electromagnetic Spectrum (Handout 12.1)
- Student Brainstorming Guide (Handout 12.2)
- Experimental Design Planner (Handout 12.3)
- Experimental Protocol (Handout 12.4)
- Sample Experimental Protocol (Teacher Resource 1)
- Laboratory Report (Handout 12.5)
- Problem Log Questions (Handout 12.6)
- Problem Log Questions (Handout 12.7)

Lesson Length

Two 60-minute sessions: one session to plan; one session to conduct the experiment and discuss

 Activities

1. Review the **Need to Know Board** and discuss why shielding would be an important concept to understand and explain at the town meeting. Shielding is an important consideration in power plant design as well as in the safe handling of any radioactive substance.

2. Discuss ways to test shielding effects on radiation. Discuss ultraviolet light as being a form of electromagnetic radiation. Students can consult the **Electromagnetic Spectrum** (Handout 12.1).

3. Show students the materials for the lesson. Divide the class into small groups and ask them to develop a method for testing the shielding properties of various substances using the materials available. Distribute copies of the **Student Brainstorming Guide** (Handout 12.2) and have the groups complete them.

4. Discuss the brainstorming results as a class.

5. Distribute copies of the **Experimental Design Planner** (Handout 12.3) and have the students complete them.

6. After they have completed the **Experimental Design Planner** (Handout 12.3), have each group write its protocol on the **Experimental Protocol** (Handout 12.4). Groups should include every step they plan to take, the materials they will use, and a data table to record their data. Students should also indicate what safety procedures they plan to use as a part of the overall experimental design.

7. Have students either work individually or in small groups to conduct the experiment. When they have finished, have them complete the **Laboratory Report** (Handout 12.5).

8. After students perform their experiments, bring the groups together to discuss their results, limitations of the results, and possible revisions in experimental design. Have students complete **Problem Log Questions** (Handout 12.6 and Handout 12.7).

9. **Ask:**

   • Was there only one way to test the effectiveness of various materials in blocking light?

   • How did you know when the light was effectively blocked?

   • Did you have any problems with your experiment?

   • What might you do differently next time?

   • Does this information help to clarify the problem? How?

   • What are some problems with this experiment as related to our nuclear energy dilemma?

 Note

   • *Safety precaution:* If a commercial research-type UV source is being used, it will be necessary for students to wear plastic UV-protective glasses; long-term exposure to UV can cause cataracts. Also, direct illumination of the skin by the UV source should be avoided; it is possible to be sunburned by these sources.

 Extending Student Learning

   • The results of the experiment will probably raise many more questions about shielding. Some small groups may want to conduct follow-up research doing additional experiments. Students should be encouraged to develop and conduct additional research.

 Assessment

   • Evaluate experiment-related forms for student understanding of experimental design.

Electromagnetic Spectrum

All of the indicated forms of radiation are identical except for wavelength and frequency.

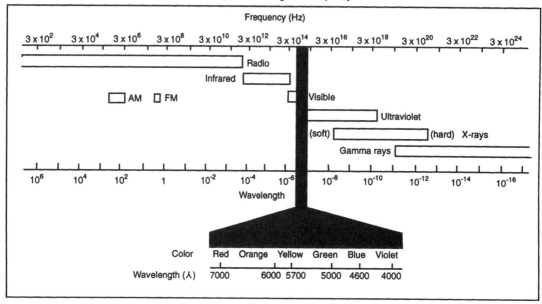

Wavelengths and Frequencies of Electromagnetic Radiation

Type of Radiation	Wavelength Range	Frequency Range
Gamma rays	$< 10^{-4}$	$> 3 \times 10^{19}$ Hz
X rays	$1 - 200 \times 10^{-8}$	$1.5 \times 10^{16} - 3 \times 10^{19}$
Extreme ultraviolet	$200 - 900 \times 10^{-8}$	$3.3 \times 10^{15} - 1.5 \times 10^{16}$
Ultraviolet	$900 - 4000 \times 10^{-8}$	$7.5 \times 10^{14} - 3.3 \times 10^{15}$
Visible	$4000 - 7000 \times 10^{-8}$	$4.3 \times 10^{14} - 7.5 \times 10^{14}$
Near infrared	$0.7 - 20 \times 10^{-4}$	$1.5 \times 10^{13} - 4.3 \times 10^{14}$
Far infrared	$20 - 100 \times 10^{-4}$	$3.0 \times 10^{12} - 1.5 \times 10^{13}$
Radio	> 0.01	$< 3 \times 10^{12}$
(Radar)	$(2 - 20)$	$(1.5 - 15 \times 10^{9})$
(FM radio)	$(250 - 350)$	$(85 - 110 \times 10^{6})$
(AM radio)	$(18,000 - 55,000)$	$(550 - 1600 \times 10^{3})$

*All wavelengths are given in centimeters; recall that 1×10^{-8} cm = 1 Angstrom; and 1×10^{-4} cm = 1 micron (10^{-6} meter)

From T. P. Snow, *Essentials of the Dynamic Universe,* 3rd ed. (Copyright 1970 by West Publishing Company).

Name   Date

Student Brainstorming Guide

1. What do we need to find out? (What is the scientific problem?)

2. What materials do we have available?

Source: Cothron, J. G., Giese, R. N., & Rezba, R. J. (1989). *Students and research*. Dubuque, IA: Kendall/Hunt Publishing Co.

continued

3. How can we use these materials to help us find out?

4. What do we think will happen? (What is our hypothesis?)

5. What will we need to observe or measure in order to find out the answer to our scientific question?

Name _____   Date _____

Experimental Design Planner

Title:

_____

Hypothesis (educated guess about what will happen):

_____

Independent variable (the variable that you change):

_____

Dependent variable (the variable that responds to changes in the independent variable):

_____

Observations/Measurements:

_____

Constants (all the things or factors that remain the same):

_____

Control (the standard for comparing experimental effects):

Experimental Protocol

1. List the materials you will need.

2. Write a step-by-step description of what you will do (like a recipe). List every action you will take during the experiment.

3. What data will you be collecting?

4. Design a data table to collect and analyze your information.

Sample Experimental Protocol
(Teacher Resource 1)

1. In a darkened room, set up a white light source (such as a lightbulb), prism, and detector (T-shirt) in such a way that light is spread out by the prism and a rainbow falls on the detector (as diagrammed on this page).

2. Place the shielding material between the prism and the detector. Turn on the lights. Observe the detector.

   • Is any light getting through?

   • Are all colors getting through?

   • Record all observations.

3. Repeat for all available shielding materials.

Data Table

Shielding material	Description of material	Description of spectrum	Shielding ability

Ultraviolet Light Experiment Diagram

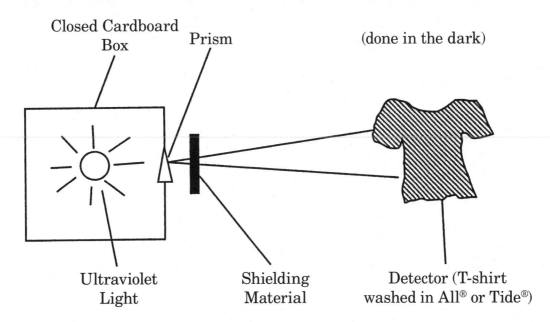

Closed Cardboard Box

Prism

(done in the dark)

Ultraviolet Light

Shielding Material

Detector (T-shirt washed in All® or Tide®)

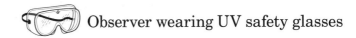 Observer wearing UV safety glasses

Laboratory Report

1. What did you do or test? (Include your experiment title.)

2. How did you do it? Cite materials and methods. You can go back to your **Experimental Protocol** (Handout 12.4) and use the information from the first two questions.

3. What did you find out? (Include a data summary and the explanation of its meaning.)

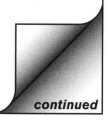

continued

4. What did you learn from your experiment?

5. What additional questions do you now have?

6. Does the information you learned help with the problem?

Name _____   Date _____

Problem Log Questions

1. Does shielding bear any importance to the topic you are investigating? If so, what is its significance? If not, why not?

2. Does this new information make the problem look different than it did previously? If so, restate the problem based on the new information; if not, state why the problem can remain as stated.

Name _____   Date _____

Problem Log Questions

Is there such a thing as a 100 percent effective shield? At what point is there too much radiation? What's the best material available now for radiation protection?

Low-Level Radioactive Waste

13

Instructional Purpose

• To infer the benefits or detriments to industries that produce radioactive waste

Curriculum Alignment    ○ Goal 1 *Concept*    ● Goal 2 *Content*    ○ Goal 3 *Process/ Experimental Design*   ○ Goal 4 *Process/ Reasoning*

 Vocabulary

Half-Life The rate of decrease of a radioactive element; the amount of time it takes for half of the atoms in a quantity of a radioisotope to decay

High-Level Radioactive Waste Radioactive materials at the end of a useful life cycle that must be properly disposed of, including the highly radioactive material resulting from the reprocessing of spent nuclear fuel, irradiated reactor fuel, and other highly radioactive material that requires permanent isolation. High-level waste (HLW) is primarily in the form of spent fuel discharged from commercial nuclear power reactors.

Low-Level Radioactive Waste A general term for a wide range of wastes having low levels of radioactivity. Industries; hospitals and medical, educational, or research institutions; private or government laboratories; and nuclear fuel cycle facilities (e.g., nuclear power reactors and fuel fabrication plants) that use radioactive materials generate low-level wastes as part of their normal operations. Low-level radioactive wastes containing source, special nuclear, or by-product material are acceptable for disposal in a land disposal facility. (Definition from http:// www.nrc.gov/reading-rm/ basic-ref/glossary/ low-level-waste.html)

Nuclear Radiation Ionizing radiation (alpha, beta, and gamma) originating in the nuclei of radioactive atoms

193

Nuclear Waste Radioactive by-products from any activity, including energy production, weapons production, and medical treatment and research

Radiation Energy emitted in the form of rays or particles that are potentially harmful to humans; it moves through space in the form of particles or electromagnetic waves

Radioactive A property of some materials whereby spontaneous emissions of alpha or beta particles or gamma rays occur; these particles and rays are potentially harmful to humans.

 ## Materials/Resources

- Chart paper
- Plain white copy paper (Handout 13.1)
- Origins of Low-Level Radioactive Waste (Handout 13.2)
- Origins of Low-Level Radioactive Waste (Teacher Resource 1)
- Origins of Low-Level Radioactive Waste reproduced on chart paper or butcher paper
- Research materials regarding low-level radioactive waste
- Internet access
- Problem Log Questions (Handout 13.2)

Lesson Length

60 minutes

 ## Activities

1. Distribute a sheet of plain white copy paper to each student. Explain to students that an isotope's half-life is the amount of time it takes for half of the atoms in a radioactive material to change into a more stable form.

2. Explain that all radioactive isotopes undergo this process but that each element decays at a different rate. These rates can range from mere seconds to billions of years.

3. Tell students that after seven half-lives, 99.22 percent of any radioactive material is in a more stable form. Tell students that after ten half-lives, 99.9 percent of any radioactive material is in a more stable form.

4. Ask students to fold their pieces of paper in half. This fold represents one half-life. Have students continue to fold the sheet in halves to represent the continually decreasing amount of radioactive material.

5. After students have completed folding their paper as much as possible, ask, What are the implications of storing radioactive material that decays in

seconds compared to the implications of storing radioactive material that takes billions of years to decay?

6. Tell students that radioactive waste comes in two forms: low-level radioactive waste and high-level radioactive waste. Ask students how long it might take low-level radioactive waste to decay. (*About 95 percent decays within 100 years or less; the remaining 5 percent decays within 500 years.*)

7. Distribute **Origins of Low-Level Radioactive Waste** (Handout 13.1). Divide students into teams of two. Tell students that they will be researching the types of industries that create radioactive waste and the products those industries create. Ask students to use the resource materials provided as well as the Internet to complete the chart **Origins of Low-Level Radioactive Waste** (Handout 13.1).

8. When student pairs have completed their investigations and their charts, call the students together for a whole-class discussion. Ask student volunteers to complete the information on the class **Origins of Low-Level Radioactive Waste** chart (on chart paper). Allow students time to make additions to their charts during this discussion.

9. Ask students to draw conclusions about the types of entries made on the chart about radioactive waste. They should be able to infer that many of the items on the chart are used to benefit people and the environment.

10. Assign **Problem Log Questions** (Handout 13.2) for class work or for homework.

 ## Assessment

- Evaluate **Origins of Low-Level Radioactive Waste** (Handout 13.1) for student ability to use reference materials to locate relevant information.

- Evaluate **Problem Log Questions** for student understanding of the origins of low-level radioactive waste.

 ## Extending Student Learning

- Apply Zeno's Paradox: ". . . in order to travel an infinite number of finite distances, which Zeno argues would take an infinite time—which is to say, it can never be completed . . ." to the concept of half-life. Write an essay describing your application of the paradox.

Origins of Low-Level Radioactive Waste

Type of Industry	Products				
Nuclear power plants					
Hospitals					
Production of new medicines					
Manufacturing industries					
Research institutions					

Origins of Low-Level Radioactive Waste
(Teacher Resource 1)

Answers may vary according to source used.

Type of Industry	Products				
Nuclear power plants	Protective clothing	Machine parts	Filters	Reactor components	Tools
Hospitals	Gloves, masks			Containers	Syringes
Production of new medicines			Paper towels	Lab glassware	
Manufacturing industries				Power supplies for space equipment	Soil testing instruments; pharmaceuticals; variety of consumer goods
Research institutions	Gloves		Paper towels	Lab glassware; lab equipment	

Problem Log Questions

1. What is low-level radioactive waste and what are its sources?

2. How hazardous is low-level radioactive waste?

3. Considering the **Problem Statement,** what are your immediate plans for ensuring the proper disposal of low-level radioactive waste?

High-Level Radioactive Waste

14

Instructional Purpose

- To discover and appreciate the problems inherent in storing high-level radioactive waste

Curriculum Alignment

 Goal 1
Concept

 Goal 2
Content

 Goal 3
Process/
Experimental Design

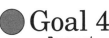 Goal 4
Process/
Reasoning

 Vocabulary

Assumption Conclusions based on one's beliefs and presuppositions

Bias A one-sided or slanted view that may be based on culture, experience, or other aspects of one's background

Half-Life The rate of decrease of a radioactive element; the amount of time it takes for half of the atoms in a quantity of a radioisotope to decay

High-Level Radioactive Waste Radioactive materials at the end of a useful life cycle that must be properly disposed of, including the highly radioactive material resulting from the reprocessing of spent nuclear fuel, irradiated reactor fuel, and other highly radioactive material that requires permanent isolation. High-level waste (HLW) is primarily in the form of spent fuel discharged from commercial nuclear power reactors.

Implication A suggestion of likely or logical consequence; a logical relationship between two linked propositions or statements

Inference Interpretation based on observation

Low-Level Radioactive Waste A general term for a wide range of wastes having low levels of radioactivity. Industries; hospitals and medical, educational, or research institutions; private or government laboratories; and nuclear fuel cycle facilities (e.g., nuclear power reactors and fuel fabrication plants) that use radioactive materials generate low-level wastes as part of their normal operations. Low-level radioactive wastes containing source, special nuclear, or by-product material are acceptable for disposal in a land disposal facility. (Definition from http://www.nrc.gov/reading-rm/basic-ref/glossary/low-level-waste.html)

Nuclear Radiation Ionizing radiation (alpha, beta, and gamma) originating in the nuclei of radioactive atoms

Nuclear Waste Radioactive by-products from any activity, including energy production, weapons production, and medical treatment and research

Perspective An attitude, opinion, or position from which a person understands a situation or issue

Point of View How people understand/look at things; what people think; the different ways people see things

Radiation Energy emitted in the form of rays or particles that are potentially harmful to humans; it moves through space in the form of particles or electromagnetic waves

Radioactive A property of some materials whereby spontaneous emissions of alpha or beta particles or gamma rays occur; these particles and rays are potentially harmful to humans.

Reasoning Evidence or arguments used in thinking

Spent Fuel Fuel that is removed from a reactor; it is highly radioactive and produces a high level of heat

Stakeholder An individual with an interest in or involvement with an issue and its potential outcomes

 ## Materials/Resources

- Chart paper
- Markers, black thin line
- Map of the United States (Handout 14.1)
- Number of Nuclear Power Plants by State (Handout 14.2)
- Reasoning Wheel (Handout 14.3)
- Reasoning About a Situation or Event (Handout 14.4)
- Political Cartoon (Handout 14.5)

Lesson Length

Two 60-minute sessions

 ## Session 1 Activities

1. Ask students to compose a definition for high-level radioactive waste and record it in their **Problem Logs.** When students have completed writing their

definition, ask for volunteers to share their writing. List common components of their definitions on the board or on chart paper or butcher paper.

2. Explain to students that high-level radioactive waste is either used fuel from nuclear power plants or waste from producing nuclear weapons.

3. Explain to students that they are going to focus on spent fuel, that is, fuel that has been used in and removed from a nuclear reactor. Tell students that spent fuel is highly radioactive and produces heat. Have students record the definition for spent fuel in their **Problem Logs.**

4. Tell students that spent fuel is usually removed from nuclear plant sites and stored in concrete vaults filled with water. Tell them that water cools the used fuel.

5. Explain that high-level radiation will lose about 50 percent of its radiation in 3 months and approximately 80 percent of its radiation in 1 year. However, it must be stored and kept isolated both from humans and the environment for thousands of years. Tell students that scientists agree that long-term nuclear storage for high-level radioactive waste will solve the problem of what to do with radioactive waste.

6. Distribute **Map of the United States** (Handout 14.1) to students. Distribute **Number of Nuclear Power Plants by State** (Handout 14.2) to every two students. Ask students to work cooperatively to plot the location of each of the operating power plants on their maps.

7. After students have plotted the location of the operating power plants on their maps, have them join in a class discussion. **Ask:**

   • What conclusions can you draw about the ratio of operating nuclear power plants on the East Coast as compared to the West Coast? To other regions of the country?

   • In which region of the country do you think underground repositories for spent fuel should be located? Justify your answer keeping in mind that this fuel must be stored for thousands of years.

   • Do you think that people in the region of the country you chose will be happy about having nuclear waste stored near their homes? Why or why not?

 Session 2 Activities

1. Explain that in this unit the students will be learning and using a certain way of thinking or reasoning. This method of thinking is something they can use in any situation, both in school and in their daily lives outside of school, and maybe even use it when talking to their parents or friends.

2. Distribute the **Reasoning Wheel** (Handout 14.3) to the students and have a copy on the board or on an overhead projector. Keep a copy of this web posted prominently in the classroom for the duration of the unit.

3. Explain to students that this way of thinking takes a while to learn and it is not going to be easy the first time. Today they are not trying to master the method; they are just getting introduced to it and they will return to it throughout the unit. Also remind students that this is just one way to help them in their thinking.

4. Work through the **Reasoning Wheel** in a question-answer format.

   • Point to the Purpose box on the web. Tell students that the first step in reasoning is to decide what your purpose is. Any time we reason or think about something, we have a goal for doing it, something we hope will be achieved or decided by our thinking; otherwise, we wouldn't waste the time to do it.

   • Direct students to the Issue/Problem oval. Explain that when thinking about something, we need to start with a clear question. Knowing exactly what we are looking for helps us to focus on important information and find an answer.

   • Tell students that once you have identified the question, you need to think about the point of view. Ask, "What do we mean when we say point of view?" (*How people understand/look at things, what people think, the different ways people see things.*)

   • When we think about something, we need to realize that there may be different ways of looking at it than our way of seeing the problem. Ask, "How could it help our thinking to look at the problem from several other people's points of view?" For example: One day you accidentally bump into your friend in the hallway and your friend gets really angry with you. You are thinking, How rude. It was an accident, and you get upset. Your friend, on the other hand, just got in a fight with a boyfriend/girlfriend or got a bad grade on a test and was in a really bad mood. Your friend just blew up but it wasn't because of what you did. (*We see things we may miss, we may realize that we don't get the problem, we may be biased, or we may learn something from another point of view, the problem may seem different/less important/more important/important for different reasons from someone else's view.*)

   • By being aware of our own point of view and trying to see others' points of view, our thinking hopefully is less biased and our arguments stronger because we have considered the way others will view the problem.

   • Next, we need to look at the evidence. Ask, "What is evidence and why is it important in answering any question?" (*It is proof/information/facts that tell you something about the question, you need it to make sure you decide the right thing, you need it to convince other people to agree with your answer.*)

   • Tell students that in reasoning we need to make sure our evidence is accurate and we need to look at evidence that supports and opposes our own ideas so that our answer is not biased.

- If students give assumptions, ask them what proof they have. Write them down and say you will come back to them. Tell students the next part of reasoning is to identify assumptions. Ask, "What are assumptions?" (*Things you think but don't have proof for, things we believe.*)

  What happens if our assumptions are weak or inappropriate and we make a decision based on them? (*We get the wrong answers; we might make a bad decision.*)

- So it is important to realize what our assumptions are and to make sure they do not lead us to a wrong answer.

- Tell students that once they have gathered data and thought about the points of view and their assumptions, they are ready for making inferences. Ask, "Does anyone know what 'inference' means or what it means to infer something?"

- Tell students that "inference" means we look at the evidence and, keeping in mind our assumptions, we conclude something from that data. For example, if we saw two crunched cars on the side of the road right next to each other and a policeman talking to people who were pointing at the cars, we would infer that those two cars had hit one another. Inferences are small steps we take in our mind about the evidence we have to help answer our question. These are tentative ideas, just suggestions to think about as possible answers. But there are degrees of inferences; some are small thoughts, while other times we have strong reactions to our inferences.

- The final step in thinking is to consider the consequences or implications of our inferences or of following through on a given point of view. Ask, "What are implications?" (*What or who will be affected by your decision, what your decision means for other people.*)

  What are consequences? (*What will happen if you do something? What are the results of your actions?*)

- Before we make a decision, we should think about who will be affected by it and what the results of our decision will be, and then think about what we should do.

5. Explain to the students that every time we reason about something we do not have to focus specifically on all these steps, because the emphasis may need to be just on some of them. Also, this is just one way to help us focus our thinking and make decisions. Tell them as they work through the unit that this will become easier and it will help them as they study nuclear energy and the issues related to its production.

6. To review the steps, have students work through them in small groups considering the **Initial Problem Statement** (Handout 3.1) to complete a **Reasoning Wheel.** Have each group take the point of view of a different stakeholder group in this situation. (This could be done as homework or in class depending on the available time.) Have students share their findings and discuss as a class.

7. Distribute **Reasoning About a Situation or Event** (Handout 14.4). Ask students to consider the issues inherent in building an underground repository for spent fuel. Have students complete the form independently.

8. Put students in groups of two or three. Ask them to compare **Reasoning About a Situation or Event** (Handout 14.4) charts. Students may wish to make additions to their charts after talking with group members.

9. Ask students what considerations they now have about the issue of repositories for high-level radioactive waste.

 Problem Logs

- Ask students to record their thinking about how they would feel if their home was located close to a nuclear plant.

- Have students brainstorm a list of considerations that must be made for creating a repository for disposal of high-level nuclear waste.

 Homework

- Provide students with a copy of the **Political Cartoon** (Handout 14.5). Ask them to analyze it and identify the stakeholders involved in decisions about adding or removing nuclear plants.

 Note

- The **Reasoning Model** introduced in this lesson, which is based on the work of Paul (1992), may be used in a variety of ways throughout the unit. The **Reasoning Wheel** can be used to consider issues and documents, and questions related to the Elements of Reasoning may be included in most lessons. You may wish to introduce the elements with reference to a current event in your school or community as a way of providing support for student understanding. In addition, using the vocabulary of the **Reasoning Model** on a regular basis can help students to learn to use the elements more effectively in considering issues. Some additional information on the **Reasoning Wheel** appears in the implementation section at the end of the unit.

 Assessment

- Evaluate the completed map of operating nuclear power plants for student understanding of locations of plants in the United States.

- Evaluate the **Reasoning About a Situation or Event** handout for an understanding of reasoning terminology.

Name _____   Date _____

Map of the United States

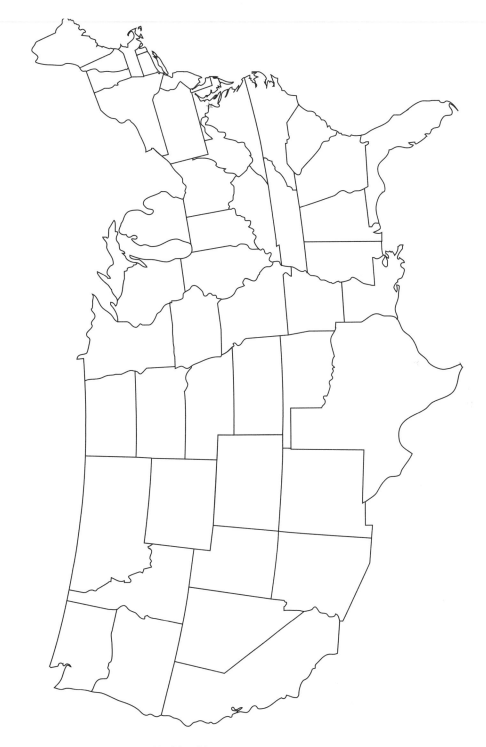

Adapted from http://geography.about.com/library/blank/usa3.jpg.

Name   Date

Number of Nuclear Power Plants by State

State	Number of Operating Plants
Alabama	5
Arizona	3
Arkansas	2
California	4
Connecticut	4
Florida	5
Georgia	4
Illinois	13
Iowa	1
Kansas	1
Louisiana	2
Maine	1
Maryland	2
Massachusetts	1
Michigan	5
Minnesota	3
Mississippi	1
Missouri	1
Nebraska	2
New Hampshire	1
New Jersey	4
New York	6
North Carolina	5
Ohio	2
Pennsylvania	9
South Carolina	7
Tennessee	2
Texas	4
Vermont	1
Virginia	4
Washington	1
Wisconsin	3

Note: Data are current as of August 2005.

Data collected from http://www.nrc.gov.

Copyright © Kendall/Hunt Publishing Company

Name _____   Date _____

Reasoning Wheel

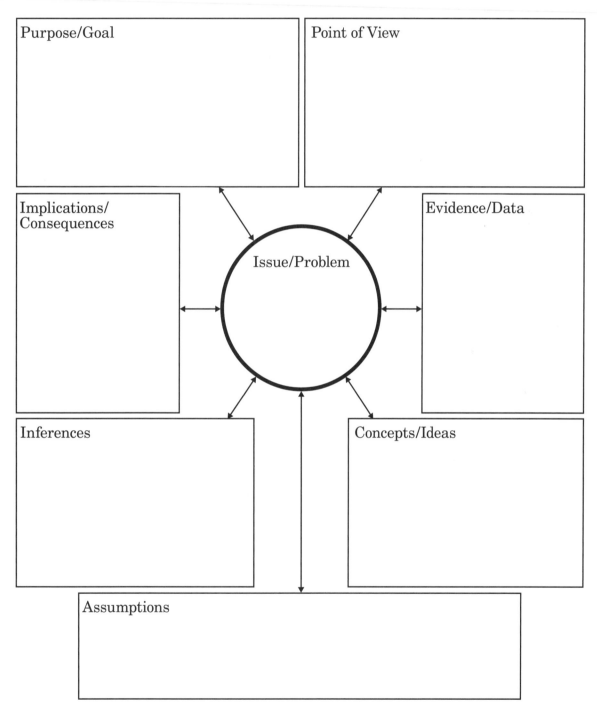

Purpose/Goal

Point of View

Implications/
Consequences

Evidence/Data

Issue/Problem

Inferences

Concepts/Ideas

Assumptions

Adapted from Paul, R. (1992). *Critical thinking: What every person needs to survive in a rapidly changing world.* Sonoma, CA: Foundation for Critical Thinking.

Name _____   Date _____

Reasoning About a Situation or Event

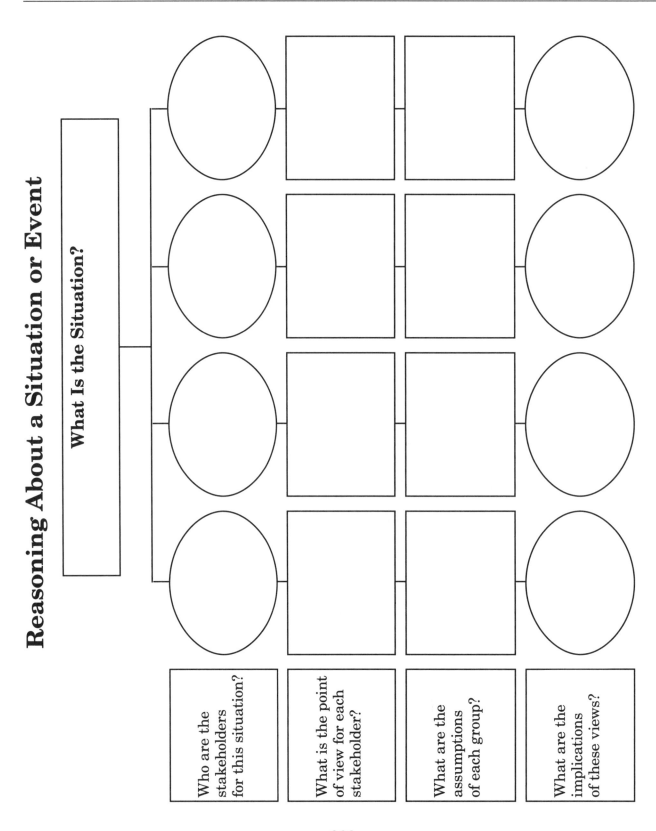

What Is the Situation?

Who are the stakeholders for this situation?

What is the point of view for each stakeholder?

What are the assumptions of each group?

What are the implications of these views?

Name _____   Date _____

Political Cartoon

© Bob Englehart/Cagle Cartoons, Inc.

http://caglecartoons.com/search.asp

15

Safety Considerations

Instructional Purpose

- To reason about situations or events that require attention to nuclear safety

---

Curriculum Alignment

 Goal 1 — **Concept**    Goal 2 — **Content**    Goal 3 — **Process/ Experimental Design**    Goal 4 — **Process/ Reasoning**

 ## Vocabulary

Assumption Conclusions based on one's beliefs and presuppositions

Bias A one-sided or slanted view that may be based on culture, experience, or other aspects of one's background

Implication A suggestion of likely or logical consequence; a logical relationship between two linked propositions or statements

Inference Interpretation based on observation

Perspective An attitude, opinion, or position from which a person understands a situation or issue

Point of View How people understand/look at things; what people think; the different ways people see things

Reasoning Evidence or arguments used in thinking

Stakeholder An individual with an interest in or involvement with an issue and its potential outcomes

 ## Materials/Resources

- Article: "Thousands of Students Stranded in Mock Safety Drill" (Handout 15.1)
- Reasoning Wheel with Prompts (Teacher Resource 1: reproduced for display in the classroom)
- Reasoning Wheel (Handout 15.2)
- Need to Know Board (Handout 15.3)
- Dagwood Model for Persuasive Writing (Handout 15.4)

Lesson Length

Two or three 60-minute sessions

 **Activities**

1. Distribute **Article: "Thousands of Students Stranded in Mock Safety Drill"** (Handout 15.1) to small groups and have students decide on a group reading strategy.

2. When student groups have completed reading the article, draw their attention to the **Reasoning Wheel with Prompts** (Teacher Resource 1), which should be reproduced on chart paper for display in the classroom. Discuss each element with students and clarify terminology.

3. When student groups have completed reading the article, ask them to complete the **Reasoning Wheel** (Handout 15.2). Student groups may help each other complete the **Wheel** or they may be completed independently; however, each student should practice using the **Reasoning Wheel.**

4. Discuss the groups' answers as a class, focusing especially on the implications of this article on your problem. **Ask:**

   • What is the central issue in this article?

   • What points of view are represented? Are there any points of view the author left out?

   • What inferences does the author draw from his data? Would you draw the same inferences?

   • How does this article relate to our problem?

   • What are the implications of this article to our problem?

5. Use the **Need to Know Board** (Handout 15.3) to organize the information that students will have to research concerning the safety of citizens in the event of a nuclear emergency.

6. Divide questions generated on the **Need to Know Board** (Handout 15.3) among groups of students and have them brainstorm ways to discover the answers to their questions. Their list should include the Internet, library research, calling the Nuclear Regulatory Commission, calling or writing to the State Nuclear Regulatory Commission, asking class resource people, and asking a nuclear engineer.

7. Give students one or two sessions to research answers to their questions and work in small groups to prepare their findings. Alternatively, assign this work as homework. After research is complete, reconvene as a large group to share answers and synthesize the information to create a "big picture." **Ask:**

   • Whose responsibility is it to ensure the safety of citizens during the event of a nuclear catastrophe?

   • Think about the map completed in Lesson 14. Is there a way to guarantee the safety of the number of people who might be affected by a nuclear emergency?

- How does one *guarantee* the safety of citizens during such times?
- Are there any local plans concerning the safety of citizens in the event of nuclear catastrophes?
- Where are the plans available?
- Compare the information that came from different sources. Was the information consistent?
- Is there a "right" side to this issue? Is one stakeholder's position more important than another's?

8. Have students write an essay using the **Dagwood Model for Persuasive Writing** (Handout 15.4) addressing the following question: Do you think that current plans concerning the safety of citizens in the event of a nuclear catastrophe are fair and adequate? Use your knowledge of nuclear power, high- and low-level nuclear waste, half-lives, and of the interconnectedness of systems to support your argument.

 Note

- The **Reasoning Wheel with Prompts** may be photocopied for individual student use as necessary.

 Extending Student Learning

- After considering many aspects of the nuclear energy problem, have students create a short poem or political cartoon illustrating the positive/negative nature of nuclear power.

 Assessment

- Evaluate student persuasive writing using the Persuasive Writing Scoring Rubric (found in *Appendix E, Suggested Rubrics*).

 Technology Integration

- Students can use the Internet to find specific information about regulations for nuclear waste disposal.

Article: "Thousands of Students Stranded in Mock Safety Drill"

By Kathryn Casa/Vermont Guardian

BRATTLEBORO—The first-ever evacuation drill designed to test plans to shuttle 1,500 schoolchildren out of Brattleboro in the event of an emergency deteriorated into chaos Thursday after nearly 40 buses simply failed to arrive.

During the drill New Hampshire emergency management officials inexplicably turned back 38 buses after bus drivers had taken the wrong road en route to local schools. That left some 1,500 students stranded for more than an hour in second-period classes at Brattleboro high and middle schools as they waited for buses that never arrived.

At approximately 11 A.M., though still nine buses short of the 30 needed for an evacuation, students were led from the school and took turns filing on and off 21 buses parked in the driveway.

The scene outside the school was chaotic. Teachers leading groups of students were confused about which buses to board. Students who had become separated from their classes stood puzzled in the middle of the sidewalk in front of the buses, asking strangers with walkie-talkies where they should go.

"I have no idea what's going on," one boy muttered to himself as students and teacher bustled past him.

"I feel safe. The alarm didn't go off," commented another boy.

Brattleboro middle and high schools are in the midst of a massive renovation and construction project, which appeared to add to Thursday's confusion. Alarms sounded in older parts of the high school building, teachers reported.

At the middle school a staff member had to go from classroom to classroom to verbally inform teachers it was time to evacuate.

A group of infants from the high school child-care center was taken outside into the freezing temperatures, where they waited a few minutes before returning to the school when their bus failed to appear. Superintendent Ron Stahley said the babies should not have been taken outside until they were assured that a bus was waiting for them.

continued

At Green Street school, meanwhile, buses pulled away from the school just as bewildered elementary schoolchildren filed out to board them after dispatchers in New Hampshire ordered the buses to return.

Local responders said the problem arose after Vermont Emergency Management officials in Waterbury failed to quickly inform their counterparts at New Hampshire Emergency Management in Concord about the number of buses needed.

New Hampshire emergency management spokesman Jim Van Dongen said Concord received a call from Waterbury at 10:25 A.M. requesting 42 buses. Concord relayed that information to the Laidlaw bus terminal in Swanzey at 10:32 A.M., Van Dongen said.

Laidlaw dispatched 41 buses and drivers, Van Dongen said.

"Our involvement in New Hampshire was fairly minimal," he added. "It was basically Vermont's drill. The buses come out of Swanzey and the request for them comes through our office."

Van Dongen said it was Laidlaw's decision to recall the buses, apparently out of concern that they would not be back in time for their regular routes.

VEM spokesman Duncan Higgins refused to acknowledge any problems with the exercise, saying only that the agency was reviewing the response. "We're still in the process of trying to put all the information together," he said.

Emergency officials in Brattleboro said they were dismayed with the drill.

"I was kind of disappointed, to say the least," said Stahley.

"It totally changed my thinking," said Jerry Remillard, town manager and chief emergency response official for Brattleboro. "I've got to admit I was one of the ones opposed to actually implementing and trying some of these scenarios. I can tell you it's not going to be like that anymore."

The drill was Vermont's first attempt to test the emergency plans to evacuate more than 3,000 children from schools and preschools within the emergency planning zone surrounding the Vermont Yankee nuclear power plant.

Emergency responders were mobilized at 9:30 A.M. after a "report" of a freight train carrying poisonous gas that derailed into the Connecticut River west of Route 142. Two cars had broken off of the train and fallen into the river, they were advised.

Stahley said things went pretty much as planned until the buses from New Hampshire, already late leaving Swanzey, inexplicably took Route 119 toward Brattleboro instead of Route 9, where police had been deployed to direct traffic.

Had the emergency been real, the buses could have been stuck in traffic along Route 119 as Hinsdale, NH, residents attempted to leave, Remillard noted.

continued

After New Hampshire officials recalled the buses, emergency officials on the ground in Brattleboro were forced to retool their plans. Laidlaw, the school bus company that contracts with our schools, reportedly pulled mechanics into service as drivers, and one Laidlaw bus broke down.

Wyatt Andrews, 17, a junior at BUHS, said he was in the school parking lot, where students with permission were allowed to evacuate to their cars. "If there was actually something that happened, kids would have been backing up and running into each other and getting in accidents," he said. "I'd rather walk to Bellows Falls. It would probably be faster."

Under the emergency plan, residents of the emergency planning zone would be evacuated to a decontamination center at Bellows Falls High School in the event of a radiological emergency.

Reasoning Wheel with Prompts
(Teacher Resource 1)

Purpose/Goal

What was the author's goal in writing this article? Do you think she accomplished this goal? Why or why not?

Point of View

What points of view are presented in this article? What biases might be present in those points of view? What points of view were omitted?

Implications/ Consequences

What are some of the implications or consequences of this article on the problem?

Issue/Problem

Students stranded during mock safety drill.

Evidence/Data

What evidence or data does the author present or contribute to the central issue? How does it contribute?

Inferences

What inferences does the author draw from her evidence? What are some inferences you can draw from the article?

Concepts/Ideas

What are some of the concepts central to the article? How does the concept of systems relate to this article?

Assumptions

What are some assumptions made by the author in writing this article? What are some made by the people she quotes?

Adapted from Paul, R. (1992). *Critical thinking: What every person needs to survive in a rapidly changing world.* Sonoma, CA: Foundation for Critical Thinking.

Name _____   Date _____

Reasoning Wheel

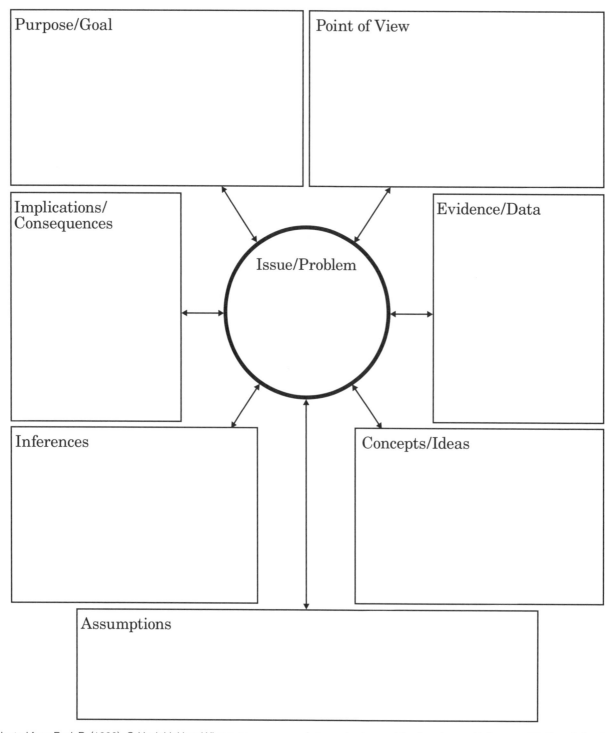

Purpose/Goal

Point of View

Implications/
Consequences

Evidence/Data

Issue/Problem

Inferences

Concepts/Ideas

Assumptions

Adapted from Paul, R. (1992). *Critical thinking: What every person needs to survive in a rapidly changing world.* Sonoma, CA: Foundation for Critical Thinking.

Name _____   Date _____

Need to Know Board

What we know . . .	What we need to know . . .	How we can find out . . .

Dagwood Model for Persuasive Writing

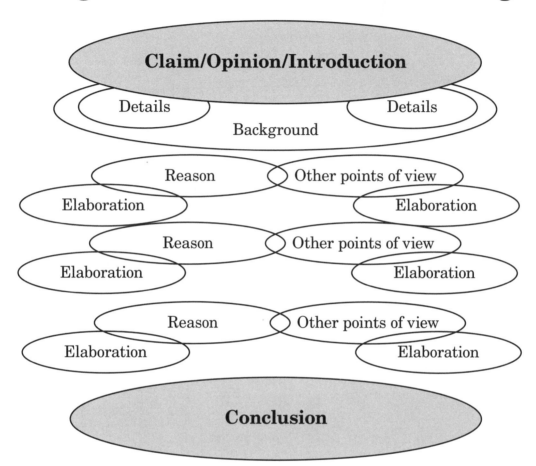

A Look at Chernobyl

16

Instructional Purpose

- To allow students to investigate the "worst case scenario" in terms of safety, biological effects of radiation, and long-term radiation effects
- To help students understand possible risks by looking at past events

Curriculum Alignment
 Goal 1 Concept  Goal 2 Content  Goal 3 Process/Experimental Design  Goal 4 Process/Reasoning

 ## Vocabulary

Nuclear Radiation Ionizing radiation (alpha, beta, and gamma) originating in the nuclei of radioactive atoms

Nuclear Waste Radioactive by-products from any activity, including energy production, weapons production, and medical treatment and research

Radiation Energy emitted in the form of rays or particles that are potentially harmful to humans; it moves through space in the form of particles or electromagnetic waves

Radioactive A property of some materials whereby spontaneous emissions of alpha or beta particles or gamma rays occur; these particles and rays are potentially harmful to humans

 ## Materials/Resources

- Article: "Chernobyl Accident: Nuclear Issues Briefing Paper 22" (Handout 16.1)
- Problem Log Questions (Handout 16.2)

Lesson Length

60 minutes

 ## Activities

1. Have students read **Article: "Chernobyl Accident: Nuclear Issues Briefing Paper 22"** (Handout 16.1) and record notes about their reactions.

2. In a large-group setting, conduct a discussion about what

students read. Allow students to explore the Chernobyl accident through the discussion. Interject only when they are going too far from the topic.

3. **Ask:**

- Please share your thoughts and feelings on what you have read.
- How is the Chernobyl incident related to our problem?
- Could the Chernobyl accident have been prevented with better safety precautions?

4. Direct the discussion toward similarities/differences of Chernobyl and the Maple Island plant.

5. Close by having students respond to the **Problem Log Questions** (Handout 16.2).

 ## Extending Student Learning

- It would be appropriate to allow more student investigations into Chernobyl if there is interest.
- Have students compare/contrast the Chernobyl accident and the Three-Mile Island accident.
- The following video is strongly recommended for viewing if it can be obtained. At present it is no longer in production, but existing copies can be obtained. It gives a firsthand look at the Chernobyl accident.

  Chernobyl: A Chronicle of Difficult Weeks. Glasnost Film Festival, Vol. #4. This is a Russian documentary film with English subtitles. Released in the United States by:

  The Video Project
  5332 College Ave., Suite 101
  Oakland, CA 94618
  1-800-4-PLANET

 ## Assessment

- Evaluate the quality of students' reasoning in their **Problem Log** responses.

Name _____   Date _____

Article: "Chernobyl Accident:
Nuclear Issues Briefing Paper 22"

March 2006

- The Chernobyl accident in 1986 was the result of a flawed reactor design that was operated with inadequately trained personnel and without proper regard for safety.

- The resulting steam explosion and fire released at least five percent of the radioactive reactor core into the atmosphere and downwind.

- 28 people died within four months from radiation or thermal burns, 19 have subsequently died, and there have been around nine deaths from thyroid cancer apparently due to the accident: total 56 fatalities as of 2004.

- An authoritative UN report in 2000 concluded that there is no scientific evidence of any significant radiation-related health effects to most people exposed. This was confirmed in a very thorough 2005 study.

The April 1986 disaster at the Chernobyl nuclear power plant in the Ukraine was the product of a flawed Soviet reactor design coupled with serious mistakes made by the plant operators in the context of a system where training was minimal. It was a direct consequence of Cold War isolation and the resulting lack of any safety culture.

The accident destroyed the Chernobyl-4 reactor and killed 30 people, including 28 from radiation exposure. A further 209 on site and involved with the clean-up were treated for acute radiation poisoning and among these, 134 cases were confirmed (all of whom apparently recovered). Nevertheless 19 of these subsequently died from effects attributable to the accident. Nobody off-site suffered from acute radiation effects. However, large areas of Belarus, Ukraine, Russia, and beyond were contaminated in varying degrees.

The Chernobyl disaster was a unique event and the only accident in the history of commercial nuclear power where radiation-related fatalities occurred.* However, its relevance to the rest of the nuclear industry outside the then Eastern Bloc is minimal.

The accident

On 25 April, prior to a routine shut-down, the reactor crew at Chernobyl-4 began preparing for a test to determine how long turbines would spin and supply power following a loss of main electrical power supply. Similar tests had already been carried out at Chernobyl and other plants, despite the fact that these reactors were known to be very unstable at low power settings.

*There have been fatalities in military and research reactor contexts, e.g. Tokai-mura.

continued

A series of operator actions, including the disabling of automatic shutdown mechanisms, preceded the attempted test early on April 26. As flow of coolant water diminished, power output increased. When the operator moved to shut down the reactor from its unstable condition arising from previous errors, a peculiarity of the design caused a dramatic power surge.

The fuel elements ruptured and the resultant explosive force of steam lifted off the cover plate of the reactor, releasing fission products to the atmosphere. A second explosion threw out fragments of burning fuel and graphite from the core and allowed air to rush in, causing the graphite moderator to burst into flames.

There is some dispute among experts about the character of this second explosion. The graphite burned for nine days, causing the main release of radioactivity into the environment. A total of about 14 EBq (10^{18} Bq) of radioactivity was released, half of it being biologically-inert noble gases. See also appended sequence of events.

Some 5,000 tons of boron, dolomite, sand, clay and lead were dropped on to the burning core by helicopter in an effort to extinguish the blaze and limit the release of radioactive particles.

Immediate impact

It is estimated that all of the xenon gas, about half of the iodine and cesium, and at least 5% of the remaining radioactive material in the Chernobyl-4 reactor core was released in the accident. Most of the released material was deposited close by as dust and debris, but the lighter material was carried by wind over the Ukraine, Belarus, Russia, and to some extent over Scandinavia and Europe.

The main casualties were among the firefighters, including those who attended the initial small fires on the roof of the turbine building. All these were put out in a few hours, but radiation doses on the first day were estimated to range up to 20,000 millisieverts (mSv), causing 28 deaths in the next four months and 19 subsequently.

The next task was cleaning up the radioactivity at the site so that the remaining three reactors could be restarted, and the damaged reactor shielded more permanently. About 200,000 people ("liquidators") from all over the Soviet Union were involved in the recovery and clean up during 1986 and 1987. They received high doses of radiation, average around 100 millisieverts. Some 20,000 of them received about 250 mSv and a few received 500 mSv. Later, the number of liquidators swelled to over 600,000 but most of these received only low radiation doses. The highest doses were received by about 1000 emergency workers and on-site personnel during the first day of the accident.

continued

Initial radiation exposure in contaminated areas was due to short-lived iodine-131, later caesium-137 was the main hazard. (Both are fission products dispersed from the reactor core, with half-lives of 8 days and 30 years respectively. 1.8 Ebq of I-131 & 0.085 Ebq of Cs-137 were released.) About five million people lived in areas contaminated (above 37 kBq/m^2 Cs-137) and about 400,000 lived in more contaminated areas of strict control by authorities (above 555 kBq/m^2 Cs-137).

On May 2–3, some 45,000 residents were evacuated from within a 10 km radius of the plant, notably from the plant operators' town of Pripyat. On May 4, all those living within a 30 kilometer radius—a further 116,000 people from the more contaminated area—were evacuated and later relocated. About 1,000 of these have since returned unofficially to live within the contaminated zone. Most of those evacuated received radiation doses of less than 50 mSv, although a few received 100 mSv or more.

Reliable information about the accident and resulting contamination was not available to affected people for about two years following the accident. This led to distrust and confusion about health effects.

In the years following the accident a further 210,000 people were resettled into less contaminated areas, and the initial 30 km radius exclusion zone (2800 km^2) was modified and extended to cover 4,300 square kilometers. This resettlement was due to application of a criterion of 350 mSv projected lifetime radiation dose, though in fact radiation in most of the affected area (apart from half a square kilometre) fell rapidly so that average doses were less than 50% above normal background of 2.5 mSv/yr.

Environmental and health effects

Several organizations have reported on the impacts of the Chernobyl accident, but all have had problems assessing the significance of their observations because of the lack of reliable public health information before 1986. In 1989 the World Health Organization (WHO) first raised concerns that local medical scientists had incorrectly attributed various biological and health effects to radiation exposure.

An International Atomic Energy Agency (IAEA) study involving more than 200 experts from 22 countries published in 1991 was more substantial. In the absence of pre-1986 data it compared a control population with those exposed to radiation. Significant health disorders were evident in both control and exposed groups, but, at that stage, none was radiation related.

Subsequent studies in the Ukraine, Russia, and Belarus were based on national registers of over 1 million people possibly affected by radiation. By the year 2000 about 4,000 cases of thyroid cancer had been diagnosed in exposed children. Among these, nine deaths were attributed to radiation. However, the rapid increase in thyroid cancers detected suggests that some of it at

continued

least is an artifact of the screening process. Thyroid cancer is usually not fatal if diagnosed and treated early.

The average radiation doses for the general population of the contaminated areas over 1986–2005 is estimated to be between 10 and 20 mSv, and the vast majority receive under 1 mSv/yr. These are lower than many natural levels.

An increased risk of leukemia due to radiation exposure from Chernobyl may become evident in the future among the higher-exposed liquidators. There is some evidence already of this and possibly solid cancers among Russian liquidators exposed to more than 150 mSv. No effect is expected in populations of contaminated areas. There is no evidence nor any likelihood of an increase attributable to Chernobyl in birth defects, adverse pregnancy outcomes, decreased fertility or any other radiation-induced disease in the general population either in the contaminated areas or further afield.

An authoritative multi-agency study published in 2005 quantified the effects. Overall some 56 people were killed or have subsequently died, including the 9 children from thyroid cancer—which could have been avoided. Among some 200,000 workers exposed in the first year, 2,200 radiation-related deaths can be expected. On the basis of statistical dose-effect models, a total of the order of 4,000 eventual deaths from the accident are possible, though most scientists involved were reported to oppose publication of such a specific estimate.

The 600-page report says that people in the area have suffered a paralyzing fatalism due to myths and misperceptions about the threat of radiation, which has contributed to a culture of chronic dependency. Some "took on the role of invalids." Mental health coupled with smoking and alcohol abuse is a much greater problem than radiation, but worst of all at the time was the underlying level of health and nutrition. Apart from the initial 116,000, relocations of people were very traumatic and did little to reduce radiation exposure, which was low anyway. Psycho-social effects among those affected by the accident are similar to those arising from other major disasters such as earthquakes, floods and fires.

The 2005 Chernobyl Forum study involved over 100 scientists from eight specialist UN agencies and the governments of Ukraine, Belarus and Russia. Its conclusions are in line with earlier expert studies, notably the UNSCEAR* 2000 Report which said that "apart from this [thyroid cancer] increase, there is no evidence of a major public health impact attributable to radiation exposure 14 years after the accident. There is no scientific evidence of increases in overall cancer incidence or mortality or in non-malignant disorders that could be related to radiation exposure."

*The United Nations Scientific Commission on the Effects of Atomic Radiation, which is the UN body with a mandate from the General Assembly to assess and report levels and health effects of exposure to ionizing radiation.

continued

As yet there is little evidence of any increase in leukemia, even among clean-up workers where it might be most expected. However, these workers remain at increased risk of cancer in the long term.

Some exaggerated figures have been published regarding the death toll attributable to the Chernobyl disaster. A publication by the UN Office for the Coordination of Humanitarian Affairs (OCHA) entitled *Chernobyl—A Continuing Catastrophe* lent support to these. However, the Chairman of UNSCEAR made it clear that "this report is full of unsubstantiated statements that have no support in scientific assessments," and the 2005 report also repudiates them.

Chernobyl today

The Chernobyl unit 4 is now enclosed in a large concrete shelter which was erected quickly to allow continuing operation of the other reactors at the plant. However, the structure is neither strong nor durable and there are plans for its reconstruction. The international Shelter Implementation Plan involved raising $715 million for remedial work including removal of the fuel-containing materials. Some work on the roof has already been carried out.

In March 2001, a $36 million contract was signed for construction of a radioactive waste management facility to treat spent fuel and other operational wastes, as well as material from decommissioning units 1–3. These will be the first RBMK units decommissioned anywhere.

In the early 1990s some $400 million was spent on improvements to the remaining reactors at Chernobyl, considerably enhancing their safety. Energy shortages necessitated the continued operation of one of them (unit 3) until December 2000. (Unit 2 was shut down after a turbine hall fire in 1991, and unit 1 at the end of 1997.) Almost 6,000 people worked at the plant every day, and their radiation dose has been within internationally accepted limits. A small team of scientists works within the wrecked reactor building itself, inside the shelter.

Workers and their families now live in a new town, Slavutich, 30 km from the plant. This was built following the evacuation of Pripyat, which was just 3 km away.

Ukraine depends upon, and is deeply in debt to, Russia for energy supplies, particularly oil and gas, but also nuclear fuel. Although this dependence is gradually being reduced continued operation of nuclear power stations, which supply half of total electricity, is now even more important than in 1986. Ukraine is also planning to develop its own nuclear fuel cycle facilities to further increase its independence.

When it was announced in 1995 that the two operating reactors at Chernobyl would be closed by 2000, a memorandum of understanding

continued

was signed by Ukraine and G7 nations to progress this, but its implementation was conspicuously delayed. Alternative generating capacity was needed, either gas-fired, which has ongoing fuel cost and supply implications, or nuclear, by completing Khmelnitski unit 2 and Rovno unit 4 in Ukraine. Construction of these was halted in 1989 but then resumed, and both reactors came on line late in 2004, financed by Ukraine rather than international grants as expected on the basis of Chernobyl's closure.

What has been gained from the Chernobyl disaster?

Leaving aside the verdict of history on its role in melting the Soviet iron curtain, some very tangible practical benefits have resulted from the Chernobyl accident. The main ones concern reactor safety, notably in eastern Europe. (The US Three Mile Island accident in 1979 had a significant effect on western reactor design and operating procedures. While that reactor was destroyed, all radioactivity was contained—as designed—and there were no deaths or injuries.).

While no one in the West was under any illusion about the safety of early Soviet reactor designs, some lessons learned have also been applicable to western plants. Certainly the safety of all Soviet-designed reactors has improved vastly. This is due largely to the development of a culture of safety encouraged by increased collaboration between East and West, and substantial investment in improving the reactors.

Modifications have been made to overcome deficiencies in all the RBMK reactors still operating. In these, originally the nuclear chain reaction and power output would increase if cooling water were lost or turned to steam, in contrast to most Western designs. It was this effect which caused the uncontrolled power surge that led to the destruction of Chernobyl-4.

All of the RBMK reactors have now been modified by changes in the control rods, adding neutron absorbers and consequently increasing the fuel enrichment from 1.8 to 2.4% U-235, making them more stable at low power. Automatic shut-down mechanisms now operate faster, and other safety mechanisms have been improved. Automated inspection equipment has also been installed. A repetition of the 1986 Chernobyl accident is now virtually impossible, according to a German nuclear safety agency report.

Since 1989 over 1,000 nuclear engineers from the former Soviet Union have visited Western nuclear power plants and there have been many reciprocal visits. Over 50 twinning arrangements between East and West nuclear plants have been put in place. Most of this has been under the auspices of the World Association of Nuclear Operators, a body formed in 1989 which links 130 operators of nuclear power plants in more than 30 countries.

continued

Many other international programs were initiated following Chernobyl. The International Atomic Energy Agency (IAEA) safety review projects for each particular type of Soviet reactor are noteworthy, bringing together operators and Western engineers to focus on safety improvements. These initiatives are backed by funding arrangements. The Nuclear Safety Assistance Coordination Centre database lists Western aid totaling almost $1 billion for more than 700 safety-related projects in former Eastern Bloc countries. The Nuclear Safety Convention is a more recent outcome.

In 1998 an agreement with the United States provided for the establishment of an international radioecology laboratory inside the exclusion zone.

The 2005 Chernobyl Forum report said that some seven million people are now receiving or eligible for benefits as "Chernobyl victims," which means that resources are not targeting the needy few percent of them. Remedying this presents daunting political problems however.

Name _____   Date _____

Problem Log Questions

1. Taking into account all that has been covered thus far, including what you know about the Chernobyl accident, how has the problem evolved? Is it the same as when you started? Has the mayor's responsibility grown?

2. With all the safety precautions we have examined, could a disaster like Chernobyl happen at the Maple Island Nuclear Power Plant? What steps could be taken to reduce the risk? Explain.

Consultation with an Expert

17

Instructional Purpose

- To provide interaction with a professional working in a radiation-related field (Suggestions for a speaker: a physician, a power plant representative, a nuclear researcher, a radiation safety officer, a representative from the Nuclear Regulatory Commission)

Curriculum Alignment
 Goal 1
Concept
 Goal 2
Content
 Goal 3
Process/
Experimental Design
 Goal 4
Process/
Reasoning

 **Vocabulary**

Radiation Energy emitted in the form of rays or particles that are potentially harmful to humans; it moves through space in the form of particles or electromagnetic waves

Radioactive A property of some materials whereby spontaneous emissions of alpha or beta particles or gamma rays occur; these particles and rays are potentially harmful to humans.

 Materials/Resources

- Chart paper and markers
- Audiovisual equipment for guest speaker
- Visitor Planning Sheet (Handout 17.1)

Lesson Length

Three 60-minute sessions

Session 1 Activities: Preparation for the Speaker

1. Brainstorm with students, deciding what questions need to be asked of the speaker. Use the **Need to Know Board** to choose questions.

2. Have students sort the questions into most- and least-important questions.

3. Students should also be guided to think about the best way to phrase the questions. Are they specific enough? Are they too specific?

4. Group questions should be recorded on a master question chart.

5. Students can then add any of their own questions to the individual **Visitor Planning Sheet** (Handout 17.1).

6. **Ask:**

   • What information do we want to know?

   • What information will the guest speaker be most qualified to give?

   • What do we want to know by the time the guest speaker leaves?

   • What facts do we want to get from this person?

   • What opinions would be interesting to have?

   • Which of these questions are most important?

   • How can we get an idea of this person's perspective on this kind of situation?

   • Do you think this person will have a bias? What would it be? How can we find out?

 # Session 2 Activities: The Guest Speaker's Presentation

1. *Guest speaker:* The guest provides his or her information regarding the area of his or her expertise.

2. Students take notes and ask their questions.

3. Students should also be prepared to share with the guest speaker background on the problem and their decisions to date.

 # Session 3 Activities: Debriefing

1. In a follow-up to the guest speaker, teacher and students should review the **Need to Know Board,** removing questions that have been answered and adding new issues, if necessary.

2. Teachers and students should discuss the potential bias in the information provided by the guest speaker and the possible effects of that bias on the validity of the information. **Ask:**

   • What were the things we learned from the guest speaker?

   • How does the new information affect our thinking about the problem?

- Do we need to reorganize our approach to the problem?
- Did this person reveal a particular bias? If so, what?
- Where can we go to get another perspective? A balanced report of information?

 **Notes**

- If the expert comes to the classroom, all students can participate. This format can also be used by small groups who need to interview an outside expert outside of class; afterward, they can report any new information to the class.
- Prior to the visitor coming to make the presentation, it would be helpful to inform him or her of the "problem" and some possible questions the students might have.

 Assessment

- Students should report information provided by the guest lecturer and reflect on the potential of bias in their **Problem Logs.**
- Have students write a thank-you letter to the guest speaker, describing which information was particularly helpful.

Name _____   Date _____

Visitor Planning Sheet

Name of Visitor:_____

Who is this visitor?

_____

_____

_____

Why is this visitor coming to see us?

_____

_____

Why is this visitor important to us?

_____

_____

_____

What would you like to tell our visitor about our problem?

_____

_____

What questions do you want to ask the visitor?

_____

_____

Nuclear Waste Management: Research on Options

18

Instructional Purpose

• To help students research and synthesize information in order to both understand a particular aspect of nuclear waste management and teach it to others

---

Curriculum Alignment    Goal 1 Concept    Goal 2 Content    Goal 3 Process/ Experimental Design    Goal 4 Process/ Reasoning

---

 **Vocabulary**

Monitored Retrievable Storage (MRS) Facility A temporary surface storage system being studied by the U.S. Department of Energy as part of an integrated system for disposing of spent nuclear fuel

 **Materials/Resources**

• Group Investigation Guidelines (Handout 18.1)
• Memorandum to the Mayor (Handout 18.2)
• Group Investigation Plan of Action (Handout 18.3)
• Group Investigation: Teacher Evaluation of Students (Teacher Resource 1)

Lesson Length

One 60-minute planning session; several research sessions

 **Activities**

1. Discuss the **Need to Know Board** in terms of waste management, focusing on the problem.

2. Provide students with a copy of the **Group Investigation Guidelines** (Handout 18.1), which should be discussed to clarify expectations for their discussion at the town meeting.

3. Present to the class **Memorandum to the Mayor** (Handout 18.2), which should set up the four topics to be researched by the groups. Once the students have read the handout, have the class divide into four groups. Each group will research one of the disposal options: on-site (storage pools or above ground), or off-site (permanent repository or MRS).

4. Have students convene in small groups to plan how they will investigate their topics. Use **Group Investigation Plan of Action** (Handout 18.3) as a guide. Students should be encouraged to web their group topics just as they did the problem. Students should be encouraged to compare the individual webs they completed in their **Problem Logs.** Webs representing a consensus among group members can be created.

5. Students should create a list of questions about their topics and think about available resources for obtaining the necessary information.

6. During subsequent sessions, groups should meet to share and synthesize information, planning how to present the information to the class. At this point, students should receive a copy of the **Group Investigation: Teacher Evaluation of Students** (Teacher Resource 1), which provides the criteria on which the students will be evaluated. The teacher may wish to modify this form to reflect school practices. Teacher and students should address during large-group sessions which information is best suited for small group instruction and which information should be presented to the class as a whole.

7. **Ask:**

   • What information will you need to present to the town about your topic to help people understand nuclear power? Why do they need to know this?

   • What will be the best sources of information for you to use to fully investigate your topic?

   • What will be the best way for you to present this information to the town?

   • Do the townspeople need to understand any other topic in order to understand yours?

   • What if the needed information is specific to a particular group? Is there any information here that everyone needs to understand?

   • What's the most efficient way of getting some of this information?

 **Notes**

1. A Research Model may be found in the *Implementation Guide.* The Research Model provides students with a way to approach an issue of significance and

explore it individually or in small groups. Its organization follows the major elements of reasoning. Teachers are encouraged to model each stage of this process in class. This model may be used to direct student research instead of the other structure described in this lesson.

2. As students investigate their nuclear energy topics and prepare for the upcoming town council meeting, they should encounter a good deal of information about nuclear energy. Students should be encouraged to gather information from a variety of sources, including print material, guest speakers, telephone interviews with local officials, and computer databases. As a general rule, the more information students get from outside sources or on their own, the better. However, if the entire class seems to need a particular body of information, the teacher may want to have a "Time Out" session in which some basic information is presented through a lecture, science demonstration, or formal experiment. Specific large-group lessons or activities should help support the topics that students are investigating and should be designed to answer **Need to Know** questions.

3. The Harvard *Project Physics* (1975) or *PSSC* (Haber-Schaim, Dodge, and Walter 1986) materials both provide much background information and interesting activities to support this content outline. Teachers should adapt activities either for small groups or for the entire class in order to respond to the **Need to Know** questions. Field trips and guest speakers provide important opportunities for students to get answers to their questions.

4. The following is a list of excellent references relating to nuclear physics, nuclear power, and/or nuclear waste management.

    Haber-Schaim, V., Dodge, J.H. & Walter, J.A. (1986). *PSSC Physics.* Lexington, MA: DC Heath & Co.

    Meller, P. (1991). Our electric future: A comeback for nuclear power? *National Geographic, 180* (2): 60–89.

    OCRUM (1990). *Science, secrecy, and America's nuclear waste: The waste management system.* Washington, DC: U.S. Department of Energy.

    Whipple, C.G. (1996). Can nuclear waste be stored safely at Yucca Mountain? *Scientific American,* June, 72–79.

Extending Student Learning

- Other areas may be investigated by students. The following topics were investigated by students in the pilot test classes:
  - Nuclear power plant design
  - Alternative energy sources
  - Government agencies associated with nuclear power
  - Accidents at nuclear power plants
  - Effects of radiation on humans and ecosystems

- Conventional uses of nuclear power
- Radioactive waste
- Advantages and disadvantages of nuclear power

 **Assessment**

- Evaluate the **Group Investigation Plan of Action** for student understanding of the task presented and the information needed.

Group Investigation Guidelines

Step 1: Choose a topic.

Step 2: WEBBING: Brainstorm information concerning the chosen topic. Include related problems that might exist. Consider "not-so-obvious" problems. Consider problems related to:

- Economy
- Politics and diplomacy
- Sociology
- News media
- Volunteer work
- Education
- Religion
- Transportation
- Health and medicine

Step 3: Develop questions you would like to have answered about the topic and tell where you would go to find the answers.

Step 4: Write a HYPOTHESIS about the topic to be investigated.

Step 5: Develop a PLAN OF ACTION to develop/test the Thesis Statement:

- Outline procedures or sequential plan of action
- Decide on deadline for the study
- Consider audience
- Consider method of presentation: written, oral, display, model, multimedia, other

Step 6: Implement the plan of action:

- Review the literature
- Collect data and record information
- Record bibliographic information
- Analyze data

Step 7: DRAW CONCLUSIONS. Examine the identified problem to see if questions have been answered. Make recommendations for further research.

Step 8: Develop a bibliography of sources throughout the research.

Step 9: Presentation of results: Time line, Poster/Charts, Oral presentations, Mural, Diorama, etc.

Memorandum to the Mayor

Acme Power
"Pioneers in the Power Industry"
Department of Waste Management

Memorandum

To: Mayor Christine Barrett's office

From: Jerry Brown, Vice President of Waste Management

Date: (date of memo)

Re: Expansion of Waste Facilities

Much discussion has risen over the planned expansion of the waste disposal pools. I realize much of the decision rests on your shoulders, and I feel it is my responsibility as Vice President of Waste Management and as your friend to inform you of alternatives to expanding the waste pools.

Expanding the waste pools is just one method of on-site disposal, but others do exist. Another possibility is an above-ground storage facility made of concrete, steel, etc. Presently, the Surry Nuclear Power Facility in Surry, Virginia, practices this technique safely and successfully.

In addition to on-site disposal, we could transport our nuclear waste to other sites across the United States. Obviously, more approvals at those sites will have to be made before any implementation. The Department of Energy is working on a permanent repository at Yucca Mountain, Nevada, and Monitored Retrievable Storage (MRS) facilities across the United States to handle the problems of storing the growing amount of the nation's nuclear waste.

I hope this information helps you work toward a good decision for all involved.

Name _____ Date _____

Group Investigation Plan of Action

Name of topic:

Web of sub-topics needed to understand topic:

Specific questions that need to be researched:

continued

Possible sources of information:

Tasks to be completed (by whom; when):

Method of presentation at town meeting:

Group Investigation: Teacher Evaluation
of Students
(Teacher Resource 1)

Name_____ Date_____

Topic_____

Evaluation Criteria

Topic/Problem _____

- Is the topic meaningful and interesting to the students?
- Is the topic "reality based"?
- Does the thesis statement provide a focus for the investigation?

Data collection _____

- Is the webbing comprehensive?
- Does the web reveal the "whole picture" concerning the general topic?
- Are the questions generated meaningful, appropriate, and are they well written?
- Are the sources selected appropriate for the topic?
- Was a variety of primary and secondary sources selected?
- Is the bibliography correctly written?

Data organization _____

- Was the data organized effectively in order to facilitate communication and understanding?
- Were visual aids relevant to the investigation?
- Does the conclusion synthesize the research?

Presentation of data _____

- Was the presentation interesting and effective?
- Did the presenter follow the group investigation guidelines discussed in class?
- Did the presenter interact with the audience effectively?

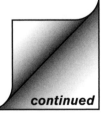

continued

Other considerations _____

- Time on task
- Student growth throughout the investigation process
- Does the investigation reflect "true research"?

Overall performance _____

Comments _____

_____

_____

_____

On-Site Storage

19

Instructional Purpose

• To provide an opportunity for students to add additional information to problem by oral presentation to the class

---

Curriculum Alignment   Goal 1 **Concept**   Goal 2 **Content**   Goal 3 **Process/ Experimental Design**   Goal 4 **Process/ Reasoning**

 ## Materials/Resources

• Oral Presentation Critique (Handout 19.1)
• Self-Evaluation (Handout 19.2)

Lesson Length

60 minutes

 ## Activities

1. Have each of the two groups researching on-site disposal methods (i.e., storage pools and above-ground storage facilities) give a 15-minute presentation on their findings to the class.

2. Once this information has been presented, refer to the **Need to Know Board** for any changes stemming from this new information.

3. Distribute the evaluation sheets to the students. All students should have the opportunity to complete **Oral Presentation Critique** (Handout 19.1) while each member of the groups presenting should also complete **Self-Evaluation** (Handout 19.2). The teacher needs to complete **Group Investigation: Teacher Evaluation of Students** (Teacher Resource 1).

4. **Ask:**
   • How does this new information fit into our problem?
   • Has the problem changed?
   • What is the most important aspect of each presentation to consider in our problem?

 **Assessment**

- Forms are provided for self-evaluation, peer evaluation, and teacher evaluation of the presentations.

 Technology Integration

- Students may use presentation software to organize and present their findings to the class.

Name _____ Date _____

Oral Presentation Critique

Peer Evaluation

Name _____ Date _____

Topic _____

Grade	0	1	2	3
1. Presentation of ideas	0	1	2	3
2. Clarity of presentation	0	1	2	3
3. Use of visual aids	0	1	2	3
4. Interaction with the group	0	1	2	3

TOTAL _____

Questions _____

_____

_____

Commendations _____

_____

_____

Recommendations _____

_____

_____

Rating scale:

0 = No points: Unsatisfactory
1 = One point: Satisfactory
2 = Two points: Extra effort
3 = Three points: Outstanding effort

Name _____ Date _____

Self-Evaluation

1. What did you like best about the investigation?

_____

_____

_____

2. What were the most interesting things you learned?

_____

_____

_____

3. Did you give your best effort to the investigation? Explain.

_____

_____

_____

4. How would you rate your overall performance? Explain.

_____

_____

_____

5. Did you use your time wisely throughout the investigation? Explain.

_____

_____

_____

Transport to Repository

20

Instructional Purpose

- To provide an opportunity for students to add additional information to problem by oral presentation to the class

Curriculum Alignment   ○ **Goal 1** Concept   ● **Goal 2** Content   ○ **Goal 3** Process/ Experimental Design   ● **Goal 4** Process/ Reasoning

 Materials/Resources

- Oral Presentation Critique (Handout 20.1)
- Self-Evaluation (Handout 20.2)

Lesson Length

60 minutes

 **Activities**

1. Have each of the two groups researching transport disposal methods (i.e., permanent repository and MRS) give a 15-minute presentation on its findings to the class.

2. Once this information has been presented, refer to the **Need to Know Board** for any changes stemming from this new information.

3. Distribute the evaluation sheets to the students. All students should have the opportunity to complete **Oral Presentation Critique** (Handout 20.1) while each member of the groups presenting should also complete **Self-Evaluation** (Handout 20.2). The teacher needs to complete **Group Investigation: Teacher Evaluation of Students** (Teacher Resource 1).

4. **Ask:**
   - How does this new information fit into our problem?
   - Has the problem changed?
   - What is the most important aspect of each presentation to consider in our problem?

Assessment

- Forms are provided for self-evaluation, peer evaluation, and teacher evaluation of the presentations.

 Technology Integration

- Students may use presentation software to organize and present their findings to the class.

Name _____ Date _____

Oral Presentation Critique

Peer Evaluation

Name _____ Date _____

Topic _____

Grade	0	1	2	3
1. Presentation of ideas	0	1	2	3
2. Clarity of presentation	0	1	2	3
3. Use of visual aids	0	1	2	3
4. Interaction with the group	0	1	2	3

TOTAL _____

Questions _____

_____

_____

Commendations _____

_____

_____

Recommendations _____

_____

_____

Rating scale:

0 = No points: Unsatisfactory
1 = One point: Satisfactory
2 = Two points: Extra effort
3 = Three points: Outstanding effort

Name _____   Date _____

Self-Evaluation

1. What did you like best about the investigation?

_____

_____

_____

2. What were the most interesting things you learned?

_____

_____

_____

3. Did you give your best effort to the investigation? Explain.

_____

_____

_____

4. How would you rate your overall performance? Explain.

_____

_____

_____

5. Did you use your time wisely throughout the investigation? Explain.

_____

_____

_____

Problem Resolution: Debate and Consensus

21

Instructional Purpose

- To use debate skills to come to problem resolution

Curriculum Alignment

 Goal 1
Concept

 Goal 2
Content

 Goal 3
Process/
Experimental Design

 Goal 4
Process/
Reasoning

 ## Materials/Resources

- Debate Format (Handout 21.1)
- Persuasive Speech Evaluation Form (Teacher Resource 1)
- Reasoning Assessment (Teacher Resource 2)

Lesson Length

Four 60-minute sessions

 ## Session 1 Activities

1. Distribute **Debate Format** (Handout 21.1) and use it to teach the skill of debating to students.
2. In Session 2 of this lesson, students will debate the following issue:

   > Resolved: That the Maple Island Nuclear Power Plant should be allowed to expand its on-site waste-storage facilities.

3. Assign the teams to be for or against the resolution. Allow students time to plan their arguments.
4. Using the procedure outlined in **Debate Format** (Handout 21.1), have the teams debate. One team debates and the other team scores and marks the argumentative points made. Reverse the roles.
5. Discuss the debate, using the **Persuasive Speech Evaluation Form** (Teacher Resource 1) and the **Reasoning Assessment** (Teacher Resource 2).
6. Refer to the **Need to Know Board** and add or change information.
7. If time permits, have students begin preparation for the problem resolution debate. Most

of the information needed for the debate should have already been covered in previous lessons.

8. **Ask:**

   - What is the difference between a debate and a discussion?
   - What is the traditional set speaking order for a debate?
   - How do you prepare for a debate?
   - How are debates judged?

 ## Session 2 Activities

1. Students will prepare for a debate on the issue:

   Resolved: That the Maple Island Nuclear Power Plant should be allowed to expand its on-site waste-storage facilities.

2. Allow one 60-minute session to prepare for the debate.

3. **Ask:**

   - What parts of the **Need to Know Board** help us support our topic?
   - If more information is needed, where can we get it?
   - What counterparts will the other team offer?

 ## Session 3 Activities

1. Begin the class with two teams debating the issue that was assigned in Session 2:

   Resolved: That the Maple Island Nuclear Power Plant should be allowed to expand its on-site waste-storage facilities.

2. Review the **Debate Format** (Handout 21.1). The teacher should be the time keeper. Teams not debating are the score keepers to encourage listening skills.

3. At the end of 15 minutes, switch team positions.

4. Score and discuss the debates.

5. Try to come to some class consensus on the problem. What is the mayor's stance going to be?

6. **Ask:**

   - What is the viewpoint of each side?
   - What position are we going to take as mayor? Why?
   - What opposes our position?

 ## Session 4 Activities

1. Have students work in their small groups to discuss the merits of both sides of the question of whether Maple Island should be allowed to expand its on-

site storage facilities. Each group should take a point of view and should write a statement for the mayor to present at the town meeting. The statement should include supporting reasons.

2. Have each group present its recommendation to the class. Discuss the recommendations and either select one (possibly with minor revisions), combine elements of several, or devise a new solution to be presented to the town council.

3. Invite a panel of interested professionals and/or parents to play the town council. Hold the town council meeting and have the mayor present the recommendation. Other students should represent various points of view of community members. Students should be prepared to answer questions from the town council.

 Notes

1. If you want students to have practice in the debate format beforehand, have them use an issue such as the following:

   Resolved: Students in our school should be required to wear uniforms.

2. Teachers may want to refer to the following article for more information on debate: Swicord, B. 1984, Summer. Debating with gifted fifth and sixth graders—Telling it like it was, is, and could be. *Gifted Child Quarterly* 28 (3): 127–129.

 Extending Student Learning

- Students can choose another related topic to research and debate if indecisions arise (such as worker compensation, the role of the federal government in decision-making, etc.).

 Assessment

- Evaluate small-group recommendations about problem resolution for their understanding of the issues and whether they have presented a well-reasoned argument.

- Evaluate student participation in the town council activity for their understanding of the issues and whether they have presented a well-reasoned argument.

Name_____   Date_____

Debate Format

What Is a Debate?

A series of formal spoken arguments for and against a definite proposal. The best solution is approved and adopted.

Debate is a special type of argument in which two or more speakers present opposing propositions in an attempt to win the audience to their sides. The teams are not concerned with convincing each other. The purpose is to try to alter the audience thinking by presenting the issues honestly with reliable evidence.

Why Debate?

Debate helps you
1. Analyze problems.
2. Reinforce statements with proof.
3. Express your ideas clearly.
4. Gain confidence.
5. Think quickly.
6. Gain a clear understanding of alternate viewpoints upon reflection.

What Are the Rules of Debating?

Debates begin with a proposed solution to a problem. The proposal should begin with the word *Resolved.* Examples:

- Resolved that the United States should abolish the electoral college and elect the president by popular vote.
- Resolved that television has beneficial effects on listeners.

1. The same number of persons speak on each opposing side.
2. Begin with careful analysis by both teams on the subject to be debated. Each member should know as much about the opponent's arguments as he or she does about his or her own position.
3. Decide which arguments are closely related and worthy of being included and which are irrelevant and should be excluded.
4. Chief points of differences between the affirmative and negative sides are the main issues.

continued

5. List the main issues for each side.

6. Find evidence that will prove the issue true or false (facts, examples, statistics, testimony).

7. Be prepared to answer the arguments of the other team's issues, called a *Rebuttal*.

What Is the Format for a Debate?

Suggested procedure:

First affirmative—Affirmative speech—5 minutes

First negative—Rebuttal—2 minutes

Second negative—Negative speech—5 minutes

Second affirmative—Rebuttal—2 minutes

The debate always begins and ends with the affirmative team. Scoring will be done by giving

1. One point for an argument

2. Two points for an argument with proof

Persuasive Speech Evaluation Form
(Teacher Resource 1)

Name_____ Date_____

Exercise_____

Directions: Use the following rating scale to evaluate each quality.
3 = Excellent   2 = Satisfactory   1 = Needs Improvement

	Needs Improvement	Satisfactory	Excellent
The purpose of the speech was clear.	1	2	3
The speaker's reasoning was clear and logical.	1	2	3
The basic components of the argument were evident.	1	2	3
The speaker showed knowledge of the subject.	1	2	3
The speaker addressed opposing points of view.	1	2	3
The speaker was audible, maintained eye contact, and spoke with expression.	1	2	3
The speaker held the interest of the audience.	1	2	3

Commendations: _____

_____

_____

Recommendations: _____

_____

_____

Reasoning Assessment
(Teacher Resource 2)

Name_____ Date_____

Directions: Please rate each student on his or her reasoning skills evidenced in oral and written communication.

3 = To a Great Extent   2 = To Some Extent   1 = Not at All

	Not at All	To Some Extent	To a Great Extent
1. To what extent is the reasoning clear?	1	2	3
2. To what extent is the reasoning specific as in citing appropriate examples or illustrations?	1	2	3
3. To what extent is the reasoning logically consistent?	1	2	3
4. To what extent is the reasoning accurate?	1	2	3
5. To what extent is the reasoning complete?	1	2	3

Commendations: _____

_____

_____

_____

_____

Recommendations: _____

_____

_____

_____

_____

Post-Assessments

22

Instructional Purpose

- To assess understanding of nuclear energy and related issues
- To assess the ability of the student to use appropriate scientific process skills in the resolution of a real-world problem
- To assess student understanding of the concept of systems

Curriculum Alignment

 **Goal 1** Concept    **Goal 2** Content    **Goal 3** Process/ Experimental Design    **Goal 4** Process/ Reasoning

---

 ## Materials and Handouts

- Content Post-Assessment (Handout 22.1)
- Content Post-Assessment Scoring Guide (Teacher Resource 1)
- Experimental Design Post-Assessment A (Handout 22.2)
- Experimental Design Rubric (Teacher Resource 2)
- Experimental Design Post-Assessment B (Handout 22.3)
- Experimental Design Scoring Guide (Teacher Resource 3)
- Systems Post-Assessment (Handout 22.4)

- Systems Post-Assessment Scoring Guide (Teacher Resource 4)

Lesson Length

Three 60-minute sessions

 ## Activities

1. Congratulate students on their success with the unit and debrief about their experiences. Have students share what they learned.

2. Distribute the **Content Post-Assessment** (Handout 22.1)

and have students complete it individually. Collect and score the assessments using the **Content Post-Assessment Scoring Guide** (Teacher Resource 1).

3. Distribute either the **Experimental Design Post-Assessment A** (Handout 22.2) or **Experimental Design Post-Assessment B** (Handout 22.3) and have students complete it individually. Score **Experimental Design Post-Assessment A** using **Experimental Design Rubric** (Teacher Resource 2). Score **Experimental Design Post-Assessment B** using **Experimental Design Scoring Guide** (Teacher Resource 3).

4. Distribute the **Systems Post-Assessment** (Handout 22.4) and have students complete it individually. Collect and score the assessments using the **Systems Post-Assessment Scoring Guide** (Teacher Resource 4).

5. Have students compare their pre-assessment responses to their post-assessment responses. Have them reflect about what they have learned and how they have grown as scientists throughout the course of the unit.

 ## Problem Logs

Have students respond to one of the following prompts:

- I want to learn more about these things in science . . .
- Studying science can help me in the following ways . . .
- When I want to know more about a topic in science, I . . .

 ## Note

- The **Post-Assessments** in this lesson are lengthy; you may wish to have students complete them over several days. However, it is important to emphasize that students should not share their ideas with each other until all three assessments are complete.

 ## Assessment

- Completed **Content Post-Assessment**
- Completed **Experimental Design Post-Assessments**
- Completed **Systems Post-Assessment**

Name _____   Date _____

Content Post-Assessment

1. Consider the following nuclear reactions:

   a. $_{92}U^{235} + _{0}n^{1} \rightarrow _{38}Sr^{90} + _{54}Xe^{143} + 3\ _{0}n^{1}$

   b. $_{92}U^{238} \rightarrow _{90}Th^{234} + _{2}He^{4}$

   Which reaction has the potential to become a chain reaction? Explain your answer.

2. Nuclear power reactors and atomic bombs both get their energy from nuclear reactions, yet nuclear power plants can't produce nuclear explosions, while atomic bombs do. What is a design feature of nuclear power plants that helps to keep them from acting like atomic bombs? How does this design feature work?

3. $_{53}I^{125}$ has a half-life of 60 days. Suppose a scientist has a sample containing 1 millicurie of $_{53}I^{125}$ today. How much $_{53}I^{125}$ will remain in her sample 120 days from now?

continued

4. Everyone is exposed to radiation during their lives. List two sources of everyday radiation exposure.

    a.

    b.

5. Unnecessary radiation exposure can be dangerous. List two health problems that radiation can cause.

    a.

    b.

6. Give an example of a piece of equipment or protective method that can protect a person against unnecessary radiation exposure, and briefly explain how it works to protect people.

Content Post-Assessment Scoring Guide
(Teacher Resource 1)

1. **(10 points)** Consider the following nuclear reactions:

   a. $_{92}U^{235} + _{0}n^{1} \rightarrow _{38}Sr^{90} + _{54}Xe^{143} + 3\ _{0}n^{1}$

   b. $_{92}U^{238} \rightarrow _{90}Th^{234} + _{2}He^{4}$

   Which reaction has the potential to become a chain reaction? Explain your answer.

   Only Reaction "a" has the potential to become a chain reaction. Reaction a uses one neutron and produces three. If conditions are right, these three neutrons can interact with three other atoms of $92U^{235}$ and cause them to fission, producing nine more neutrons, which can then go on to cause even more fission events. . . A reaction whose products have the potential to cause more reactions like it is called a chain reaction.

   Give **5 points** for the right answer and **5 points** for the right explanation.

2. **(10 points)** Nuclear power reactors and atomic bombs both get their energy from nuclear reactions, yet nuclear power plants can't produce nuclear explosions, while atomic bombs do. What is a design feature of nuclear power plants that helps to keep them from acting like atomic bombs? How does this design feature work?

   Examples include:

   Fuel rod design: Keeps the reaction from proceeding too quickly by keeping the fissile atoms (material that is capable of undergoing fission) well-enough separated from each other.

   Presence of a moderator: Moderators are substances that absorb neutrons to slow the progress of the chain reaction; control rods are made of such substances.

   Note: The containment building is not an acceptable answer to this question. While it is a safety device, it has nothing to do with the chain reactions occurring inside.

   Give **5 points** for the design feature and **5 points** for the explanation.

3. **(5 points)** $_{53}I^{125}$ has a half-life of 60 days. Suppose a scientist has a vial containing 1 millicurie of $_{53}I^{125}$ today. How much $_{53}I^{125}$ will remain in her vial 120 days from now?

   120 days is two half-lives: Thus, one-quarter, or 0.25 mCi, of $_{53}I^{125}$ will remain in her vial.

   Give **5 points** for the correct answer.

4. **(10 points)** Everyone is exposed to radiation during their lives. List two sources of everyday radiation exposure.

   The sun (ultraviolet rays and cosmic rays); radioactive elements naturally present in the world around us (in soil, water, air, and our own bodies); medical treatments (X-rays and radiation therapy, for example).

   Give **5 points** for each correct answer.

5. **(10 points)** Unnecessary radiation exposure can be dangerous. List two kinds of health problems that radiation can cause.

   Cancer, cataracts, genetic defects, radiation burns, sunburn.

   Give **5 points** for each correct answer.

6. **(5 points)** Give an example of a piece of equipment or protective method that can protect a person against unnecessary radiation exposure, and briefly explain how it works to protect people.

   Sunscreen; lead aprons at the dentist's, water in a nuclear fuel rod storage pool: All act as shielding materials because they absorb various kinds of radiation.

   Geiger counters and film badges: These items act as detection devices that allow a person to determine whether he or she is being exposed to dangerous radiation levels.

   Give **2.5 points** for a correct item and **2.5 points** for a correct explanation.

   Total number of points possible: 50

Name _____   Date _____

Experimental Design Post-Assessment A

Construct a fair test of the following question: Is the speed of a nuclear reaction always constant or does it vary?

Describe in detail how you would test this question. Be as scientific as you can as you write about your test. Write the steps you would take to determine whether the speed of a nuclear reaction is always constant or whether it varies.

Adapted from Fowler, M. (1990) The diet cola test, *Science Scope 13(4)*, 32–34.

Teacher Resource 2: Experimental Design Rubric

Criteria	Strong Evidence 2	Some Evidence 1	No Evidence 0	Pre	Post
States **PROBLEM** or **QUESTION.**	Clearly states the problem or question to be addressed.	Somewhat states the problem or question to be addressed.	Does not state the problem or question to be addressed.		
Generates a **PREDICTION** and/or **HYPOTHESIS.**	Clearly generates a prediction or hypothesis appropriate to the experiment.	Somewhat generates a prediction or hypothesis appropriate to the experiment.	Does not generate a prediction or hypothesis.		
Lists experiment steps.	Clearly & concisely lists four or more steps as appropriate for the experiment design.	Clearly & concisely lists one to three steps as appropriate for the experiment design.	Does not generate experiment steps.		
Arranges steps in **SEQUENTIAL** order.	Lists experiment steps in sequential order.	Generally lists experiment steps in sequential order.	Does not list experiment steps in a logical order.		
Lists **MATERIALS** needed.	Provides an inclusive and appropriate list of materials.	Provides a partial list of materials needed.	Does not provide a list of materials needed.		
Plans to **REPEAT TESTING** and tells reason.	Clearly states a plan to conduct multiple trials, providing reasoning.	Clearly states a plan to conduct multiple trials.	Does not state plan or reason to repeat testing.		
DEFINES the terms of the experiment.	Correctly defines all relevant terms of the experiment.	Correctly defines some of the relevant terms of the experiment.	Does not define terms, or defines terms incorrectly.		
Plans to **MEASURE.**	Clearly identifies plan to measure data.	Provides some evidence of planning to measure data.	Does not identify plan to measure data.		
Plans **DATA COLLECTION.**	Clearly states plan for data collection, including note-taking, the creation of graphs or tables, etc.	States a partial plan for data collection.	Does not identify a plan for data collection.		
States plan for **INTERPRETING DATA.**	Clearly states plan for interpreting data by comparing data, looking for patterns and reviewing previously known information.	States a partial plan for interpreting data.	Does not state plan for interpreting data.		
States plan for drawing a **CONCLUSION BASED ON DATA.**	Clearly states plan for drawing conclusions based on data.	States a partial plan for drawing conclusions based on data.	Does not state plan for drawing conclusions.		
			TOTAL SCORE:		

Adapted from Fowler, M. (1990). The diet cola test. *Science Scope, 13(4)*, 32–34.

Experimental Design Post-Assessment B

You are a biologist, working in a university medical research laboratory that uses small amounts of $_{15}P^{32}$, a radioactive isotope of phosphorous that has a 14-day half-life and is easily shielded with plexiglass. The experiments that you do result in the production of low-level liquid radioactive waste. The liquid waste is stored for later removal in plastic gallon jugs. There is a liquid waste bottle that is kept behind a plexiglass shield on the floor next to your lab bench. For the sake of convenience and to prevent spills, there is a funnel in the neck of the waste bottle; this allows you to safely pour your radioactively contaminated liquids into the jug. The waste bottle is not usually capped; you believe that this is safe, because the radioactive materials that you are using are not volatile (in other words, they won't leave the bottle and contaminate the air.)

Late one night, as you are finishing a long experiment, you notice something disconcerting: a large, brown cockroach has crawled out of the liquid waste bottle and is teetering on the top edge of the funnel. Quickly, you trap the roach in a jar. You take the roach down the hall to the scintillation counter, a machine that will allow you to determine whether the roach contains $_{15}P^{32}$ and, if so, how much. Scintillation counting reveals that the roach (who had to be sacrificed for the sake of the experiment) was, indeed, contaminated with high levels of $_{15}P^{32}$.

You had known that the building was roach-infested, but the possibility that the roaches would drink your radioactive liquid waste had not occurred to you before. You begin to wonder how many other cockroaches have visited your waste bottle. Describe an experiment that will allow you to decide whether radioactive cockroaches pose a contamination problem in your building.

In your answer, include the following:

a. Your hypothesis

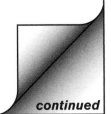

continued

b. The materials you would need

c. The protocol you would use

d. A data table showing what data you would collect

e. A description of how you would use your data to decide whether radioactive roaches did indeed pose a contamination problem for the lab building

Experimental Design Scoring Guide
(Teacher Resource 3)

Describe an experiment that will allow you to decide whether radioactive cockroaches pose a contamination problem in your building. In your answer, include the following:

a. **(5 points)** Your hypothesis:

You have already found one highly radioactive roach. If other roaches had also been drinking out of the radioactive waste bottle, they would be radioactive too. Because the waste bottle was open and available to roaches, and because the building is roach-infested, I hypothesize that many other roaches in the building will prove to be highly radioactive, which will indeed be a contamination problem.

Note: Other hypotheses are possible; accept all reasonable answers; give **5 points** for any reasonable hypothesis.

b. **(10 points)** The materials you would need, including any necessary safety equipment:

Scintillation counter and related analyzing equipment
Roach motels
Jars to keep the roaches in, once captured
Jugs for liquid radioactive waste
Waste cans for solid radioactive waste
Plexiglass shielding

Note: The student only needs to list the detector for radioactive material **(3 points)**, plexiglass shielding to protect himself or herself against possible radiation exposure from the roaches **(4 points)**, and the roaches themselves **(3 points)**: This materials list does not need to be comprehensive.

Note: Accept all reasonable materials lists, as long as they're consonant with the hypothesis in Part a.

c. **(10 points)** The protocol you would use:

As a single, captured, radioactive roach by itself does not constitute a problem, I would need to capture a large number of roaches in the building and check each of them in the scintillation counter in order to determine whether there was indeed a major contamination problem. Accordingly, I would place roach motels in dark places along the baseboards in every room and hallway in the building. I would leave the roach motels for a few days in order to maximize my capture rate; I would then collect the roach motels, being careful to label each one to indicate where the roaches in it were captured. All roaches and roach by-products would be stored behind plexiglass shields in order to minimize my possible radiation exposure during this experiment. I would then run each captured roach through the scintillation counter (a process that they, alas, would not survive) in order to determine how radioactive they are. As a negative control, I would also capture and count roaches in a place where no radioactive materials are used, such as my graduate student apartment.

Give **5 points** for any protocol (or experimental outline: Not every step need be listed in fine detail, but it should be clear what the student intends to test) that is consonant with the hypothesis given in Part a (if the two seem to be unrelated, withhold these points); give **5 points** for the presence of a control for the experiment.

d. (**15 points**) A data table showing what data you would collect:

Location   Roach I.D. # $_{15}P^{32}$ counts per minute

Note: Accept all reasonable answers, as long as they are consonant with the student's answers to parts a–d.

Give **5 points** for the presence of a data table; **5 points** if there is an independent variable (not necessarily labeled as such) present in the data table headings; and **5 points** if there is at least one dependent variable (not necessarily labeled as such) present in the data table headings. In this answer, roach location is the independent variable, and counts per minute is the dependent variable.

e. (**10 points**) A description of how you would use your data to decide whether radioactive roaches did indeed pose a serious contamination problem for the lab building:

In order to be safe, the roaches would have to contain no more $_{15}P^{32}$ than the background level present in the control roaches from my apartment. If they contained significantly more of the isotope than this, and if many roaches from many parts of the building were found to be contaminated, then I would say that the roaches pose a significant contamination problem. I would thus compare the results from the lab roaches with those from the apartment roaches and see if the lab roaches were indeed significantly more radioactive than the apartment roaches.

Note: Accept all reasonable answers, as long as they are consonant with the student's answers to parts a–d.

Give **10 points** for an answer that explains how the data will be used to come up with a conclusion. If the student doesn't mention the data, then give no points.

Total number of points possible: 50

Name _____   Date _____

Systems Post-Assessment

A storage facility for spent nuclear reactor fuel can be thought of as a system.

1. List the parts of the system. Include boundaries, elements, input, and output.

   Boundaries (describe):

   Elements (list at least five):

   Inputs (list at least two kinds):

   Outputs (list at least two kinds):

continued

2. Draw a diagram of the system that shows where each of the parts can be found.

3. On your diagram in the preceding question, draw lines (in a different color) showing three important interactions between different parts of the system. Why is each of these interactions important to the system? Explain your answer.

   a. Interaction 1:

   b. Interaction 2:

   c. Interaction 3:

Systems Post-Assessment Scoring Guide
(Teacher Resource 4)

A storage facility for spent nuclear reactor fuel can be thought of as a system. For this system, do the following:

1. **(25 points)** List the parts of the system. Include boundaries, elements, input, and output.

   Boundaries (describe):

   The boundaries of this system are the boundaries of the storage building.

   For **10 points** total, accept any reasonable *closed* boundaries, but be sure that the elements, input, and output listed are consistent with them.

   Elements (list at least five):

   Fuel rods and their parts, including fuel and casing materials; the water in the storage pond; the cement that makes up the pool's walls; the air in the storage building.

   Give **1 point** for each reasonable element up to a maximum of **5 points.**

   Input (list at least two kinds):

   Air from outside the storage building, insects from outside the storage building, workers and machinery, more depleted fuel rods.

   Give **2.5 points** for each listed input item up to a maximum of **5 points.**

   Output (list at least two kinds):

   Air leaving the storage building, insects leaving the storage building, workers and equipment leaving the storage building, water leaking through cracks in the cement of the pool, fuel rods headed for a more permanent repository.

   Give **2.5 points** for each listed output item, up to **5 points.**

2. **(10 points)** Draw a diagram of the system that shows where each of the parts can be found.

   Accept any reasonable diagram.

3. **(15 points total)** On your diagram, draw lines (in a different color) showing three important interactions between different parts of the system. Why is each of these interactions important to the system? Explain your answer.

    a. Interaction 1:

    Water absorbing neutrons produced by the fuel rods: Water acts as shielding material.

    b. Interaction 2:

    Radiation and cement walls of storage pool: gradually can reduce the strength of the cement; cement also acts as a shielding material.

    c. Interaction 3:

    Radiation from decay of fuel interacts with fuel rod casings to reduce their strength.

    Accept any reasonable interaction; give **5 points** for each correct answer.

    Total number of points possible: 50

3

Implementation Guidelines

Implementation Guidelines

The following pages provide guidelines for teachers to implement this unit effectively in classrooms, including some design and logistical discussions. Copies and explanations of the teaching models are also included.

1. Implementation Considerations

Target Population

This unit was designed to serve the learning needs of highly able students in the middle grades (6 to 8). Lessons have been piloted both in classes for the gifted and in heterogeneous settings, with teachers modifying some reading selections and activities for use with some students as appropriate.

Alignment of the Unit with Standards

The unit was designed to align with standards set forth by the *National Science Education Standards* and the *Benchmarks for Science Literacy* with regard to process, content, and concept elements, including emphases on logical thinking, data collection and interpretation, and experimental design. The unit also supports student learning in other areas, particularly in the language arts area of persuasive writing.

Schedule for Unit Implementation

Recognizing the limited time often allotted to science in the school schedule, lessons incorporated in this unit might require more than one class period to implement. Teacher judgment is recommended as to where to split the lessons.

Use of Technology

Internet access and other technological tools will provide support for unit implementation and enhance the experience for students and teachers. A number of Internet sites are listed in *Part 4, Appendix B, Suggested Mini-Lessons*. In addition, the Internet is a useful resource for completing the unit activities. Beyond this, computers should be utilized to support student word-processing skills on writing assignments in the unit, and presentation software may be used in project development. Additional technology integration suggestions are listed with lessons where appropriate.

Collaboration with Media Specialists

The exploration of science concepts can be considerably enhanced for students through the use of resources that bring science alive through pictures and stories. Moreover, nonfiction resources support both teacher and student knowledge about systems. Teachers and media specialists can work together to collect such resources and have them available in the classroom or media center during the implementation of the unit. Some of the resources recommended in this unit may not be available at school libraries but may be found in public or university libraries, and specialists at these institutions can be very helpful as well in collecting listed resources and recommending additional ones. *Appendix D, Supplemental Readings for Students* lists both fiction and nonfiction texts for students.

Students should also be encouraged to utilize their library/media centers and to become acquainted with the librarians in their community for several reasons. First, libraries are complex systems of organizing information. The systems vary from one library to another, and technological access to the systems is constantly changing. Media specialists serve as expert guides to the information maze and they are eager to assist library users. Second, the most important skill in using the library is knowing how to ask questions. Students should learn that working with a media specialist is not a one-time inquiry or plea for assistance but an interactive communication and discovery process. As the student asks a question and the media specialist makes suggestions, the student will gain a better understanding of the topic and find new questions and ideas to explore. To maximize the use of library resources, the student should then discuss these new questions and ideas with the media specialist. Learning to use the services of media specialists and other information professionals is an important tool for lifelong learning.

2. Learning Centers

Learning centers can serve as useful tools throughout this unit to give students more opportunities to explore the unit's topics and to deepen their understanding. A few suggestions for learning centers follow.

Writing Center

Students may work at a writing center to strengthen their persuasive writing skills throughout the unit. They may use the writing center to revise and edit assignments given in the lessons or to practice writing in response to other prompts provided. Copies of the Hamburger Model for Persuasive Writing (or Dagwood Model for more able students), dictionaries, and thesauruses should be available at the writing center for students to reference.

Computer Center

A computer center may be used in several different ways during this unit. Students may use computer time for writing and editing or for working on their research projects for this unit. In addition, relevant websites involving nuclear energy may be bookmarked for students to visit and explore.

Map Analysis Center

At this center, maps should be available to students for additional study. Students may conduct research regarding worldwide locations for power plants and plans for future nuclear power plants. They may analyze the locations for proposed plants relative to their proximity to human inhabitants and natural resources.

Nuclear Energy History Center

Provide electronic and print copies of materials related to the history of nuclear energy. Have students develop a time line of important events to display in the classroom.

Nuclear Energy in the News Center

Gather materials from recent news articles regarding the use of nuclear energy for powering homes and businesses. Students may use the materials to develop presentations or other products to demonstrate their understanding of the issues for and against nuclear energy.

3. Teaching Models

A. The Taba Model for Concept Development

This model is introduced in Lesson 3 of the unit. The concept of systems is used as an organizer throughout the unit, with numerous questions and activities that explore students' understanding of the concept and the generalizations. This model is based on the work of Taba (1962).

The model as described here may be applied with various concepts and with students at various grade and ability levels.

Use the following questions to guide an introductory discussion about systems. In groups, students should discuss the questions and record ideas on large sheets of paper for sharing with the class. Each section of the small-group activity should be followed by a brief whole-class discussion.

Brainstorm ideas about systems and write down all responses.
- What words come to mind when you think about systems?
- What are some examples of systems? What is it about them that makes them systems?
- How do you decide whether something is a system?

Categorize the ideas that were written down, grouping them, and giving each group a title.
- How would you categorize these ideas into groups?
- What could you call each group? Why?
- Do all of your systems fall into groups? Might some of them belong in more than one group? How else might you group your ideas?
- What are some of the characteristics of systems, based on the ideas you wrote?

Brainstorm a list of things that are not systems.
- What are some examples of things that are not systems?
- What evidence or proof do you have that these things are not systems?

- How might you group the things that are not systems? What can you call each of these groups?
- How are the groups of things that are not systems similar to or different from the groups of things that are systems? Are there patterns to your groupings?

Make generalizations about systems.

A generalization is something that is always or almost always true. What can you say about systems that are always or almost always true? Use your examples and categories to guide your thinking and write several statements that are generalizations about systems.

Sample Systems Diagram

System: Fish Tank

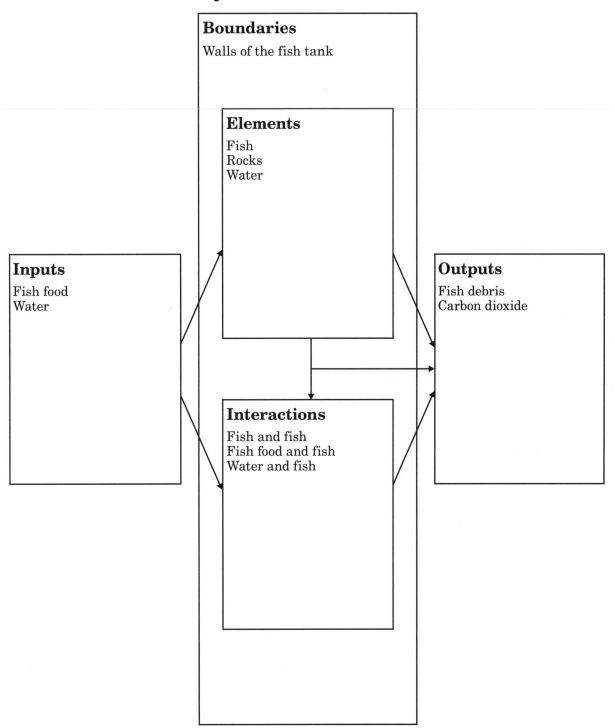

Boundaries

Walls of the fish tank

Elements

Fish
Rocks
Water

Inputs

Fish food
Water

Outputs

Fish debris
Carbon dioxide

Interactions

Fish and fish
Fish food and fish
Water and fish

B. The Hamburger and Dagwood Models for Persuasive Writing

The purpose of the Hamburger Model is to provide students with a useful metaphor to aid them in developing a persuasive paragraph or essay. The model should be introduced by the teacher, showing students that the top bun and the bottom bun represent the introduction and conclusion of any persuasive writing piece. The teacher should note that the reasons given in support of the thesis statement are like the meat or vegetables in a hamburger, providing the major substance of the sandwich. Elaboration represents the condiments in a sandwich—the ketchup, mustard, and onions that enhance the sandwich's appeal—just as examples and illustrations enhance the appeal of a written persuasive writing piece.

Teachers should show students examples of hamburger paragraphs and essays and have students find the top bun, bottom bun, hamburger, and condiments. Students should have opportunities to evaluate the quality of the different components and the essay as a whole.

Teachers may ask students to construct their own hamburger paragraphs. After students have constructed their own paragraphs, teachers may use peer and self-assessments to have students judge their own and one another's writing. This process should be repeated throughout the unit.

The Dagwood Model is an elaborated version of the Hamburger Model that uses the familiar metaphor of a sandwich to help students construct a paragraph or essay. Students begin by stating their point of view on the issue in question (the top bun). They then provide reasons, or evidence, to support their claim; they should try to incorporate at least three supportive reasons (the "patties"). Elaboration on the reasons provides additional detail (the "fixings"). A concluding sentence or paragraph wraps up the sandwich (the bottom bun). The Dagwood Model also asks students to introduce and refute other points of view.

The following pages demonstrate both versions of the model in graphic formats.

Hamburger Model for Persuasive Writing
(Version Including Elaboration)

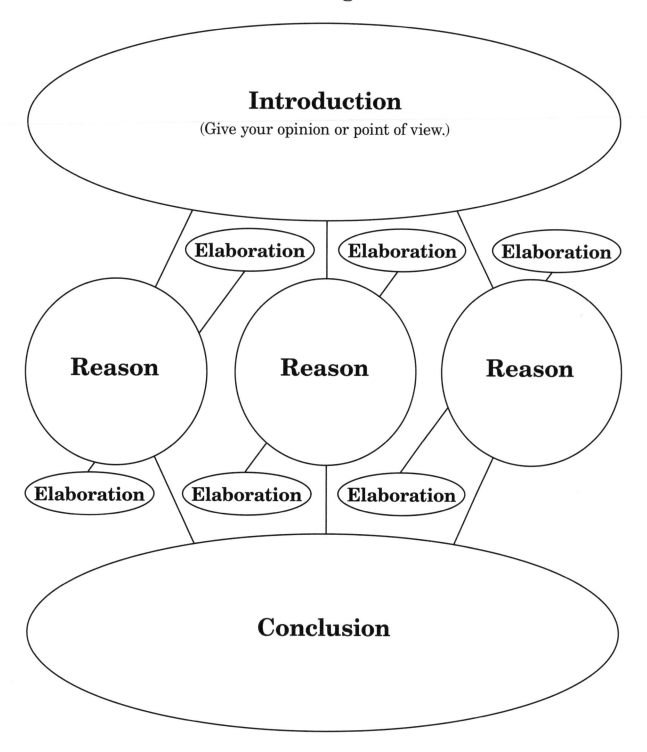

Introduction
(Give your opinion or point of view.)

Elaboration

Elaboration

Elaboration

Reason

Reason

Reason

Elaboration

Elaboration

Elaboration

Conclusion

Dagwood Model for Persuasive Writing

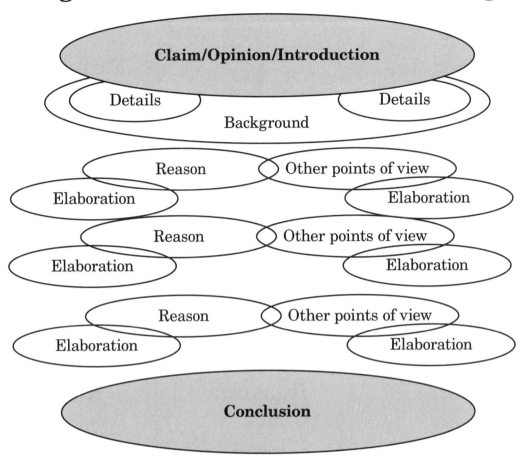

C. Elements of Reasoning

The reasoning strand used throughout this unit focuses on eight elements of thought identified by Richard Paul (1992). It is embedded in most lessons of the unit through questions, writing assignments, and research work. These elements of thought are the basic building blocks of productive thinking. Working together, they provide a general logic to reasoning. In document interpretation and listening, they help one make sense of the reasoning of the author or speaker. In writing and speaking, they enable authors or speakers to strengthen their arguments. In this unit for primary students, only some of the elements are introduced specifically, while others are only touched on through questions. This unit gives students an introduction to the elements that can be followed up in future units of study.

Students are often asked to distinguish between facts and opinions. However, between pure opinion and hard facts lie reasoned judgments in which beliefs are supported by reasons.

1. **Purpose, Goal, or End View:** We reason to achieve some objective, to satisfy a desire, to fulfill some need. For example, if the car does not start in the morning, the purpose of my reasoning is to figure out a way to get to work. One source of problems in reasoning is traceable to defects at the level of purpose or goal. If our goal itself is unrealistic, contradictory to other goals we have, confused or muddled in some way, then the reasoning we use to achieve it is problematic. If we are clear on the purpose for our writing and speaking, it will help focus the message in a coherent direction. The purpose in our reasoning might be to persuade others. When we read and listen, we should be able to determine the author's or speaker's purpose.

2. **Question at Issue (or Problem to Be Solved):** When we attempt to reason something out, there is at least one question at issue or problem to be solved (if not, there is no reasoning required). If we are not clear about what the question or problem is, it is unlikely that we will find a reasonable answer, or one that will serve our purpose. As part of the reasoning process, we should be able to formulate the question to be answered or the issue to be addressed. For example, why won't the car start? Or, should libraries censor materials that contain objectionable language?

3. **Points of View or Frame of Reference:** As we take on an issue, we are influenced by our own point of view. For example, parents of young children and librarians might have different points of view on censorship issues. The price of a shirt may seem too low to one person while it seems high to another because of a different frame of reference. Any defect in our point of view or frame of reference is a possible source of problems in our reasoning. Our point of view may be too narrow, may not be precise enough, may be unfairly biased, and so forth. By considering multiple points of view, we may sharpen or broaden our thinking. In writing and speaking, we may strengthen our arguments by acknowledging other points of view. In listening and reading,

we need to identify the perspective of the speaker or author and understand how it affects the message delivered.

4. **Experiences, Data, Evidence:** When we reason, we must be able to support our point of view with reasons or evidence. Evidence is important in order to distinguish opinions from reasons or to create a reasoned judgment. Evidence and data should support the author's or speaker's point of view and can strengthen an argument. An example is data from surveys or published studies. In reading and listening, we can evaluate the strength of an argument or the validity of a statement by examining the supporting data or evidence. Experiences can also contribute to the data of our reasoning. For example, previous experiences in trying to get a car to start may contribute to the reasoning process that is necessary to solve the problem.

5. **Concepts and Ideas:** Reasoning requires the understanding and use of concepts and ideas (including definitional terms, principles, rules, or theories). When we read and listen, we can ask ourselves, "What are the key ideas presented?" When we write and speak, we can examine and organize our thoughts around the substance of concepts and ideas. Some examples of concepts are freedom, friendship, and responsibility.

6. **Assumptions:** We need to take some things for granted when we reason. We need to be aware of the assumptions we have made and the assumptions of others. If we make faulty assumptions, this can lead to defects in reasoning. As a writer or speaker we make assumptions about our audience and our message. For example, we might assume that others will share our point of view, or we might assume that the audience is familiar with the First Amendment when we refer to "First Amendment rights." As a reader or listener, we should be able to identify the assumptions of the writer or speaker.

7. **Inferences:** Reasoning proceeds by steps called *inferences*. An inference is a small step of the mind, in which a person concludes that something is so because of something else being so or seeming to be so. The tentative conclusions (inferences) we make depend on what we assume as we attempt to make sense of what is going on around us. For example, we see dark clouds and infer that it is going to rain, or we know the movie starts at 7:00, it is now 6:45, and it takes 30 minutes to get to the theater, so we cannot get there on time. Many of our inferences are justified and reasonable, but many are not. We need to distinguish between the raw data of our experiences and our interpretations of those experiences (inferences). Also, the inferences we make are heavily influenced by our point of view and assumptions.

8. **Implications and Consequences:** When we reason in a certain direction, we need to look at the consequences of that direction. When we argue and support a certain point of view, solid reasoning requires that we consider

what the implications are of following that path; what are the consequences of taking the course that we support? When we read or listen to an argument, we need to ask ourselves what follows from that way of thinking. We can also consider consequences of actions that characters in stories take. For example, if I do not do my homework, I will have to stay after school to do it; if I water the lawn, it will not wither in the summer heat.

Reasoning Wheel

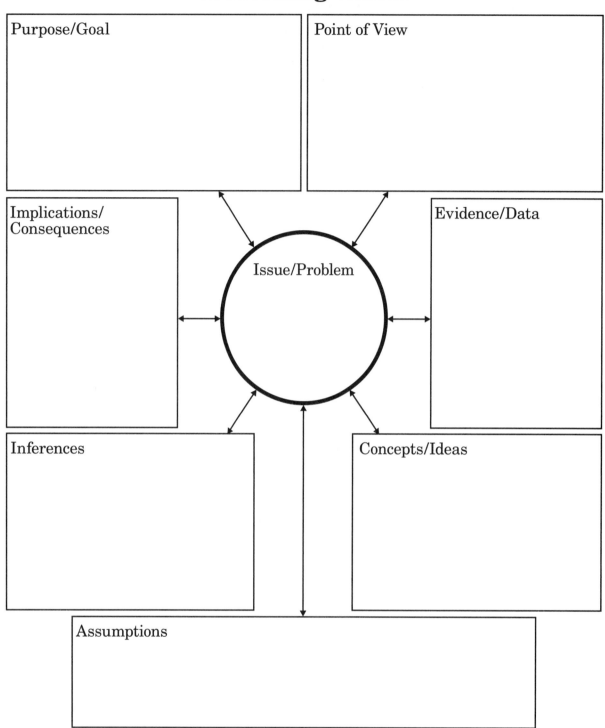

Purpose/Goal

Point of View

Implications/
Consequences

Evidence/Data

Issue/Problem

Inferences

Concepts/Ideas

Assumptions

Adapted from Paul, R. (1992). *Critical thinking: What every person needs to survive in a rapidly changing world.* Sonoma, CA: Foundation for Critical Thinking.

Sample Reasoning Wheel

Purpose/Goal/End view

What is the purpose of discussing this issue as it relates to the problem situation?

Point of View/Frame of Reference

From what perspective do you approach the issue? What interest groups or stakeholders may have different points of view on the topic of the most effective response? What might their viewpoints be?

Implications/Consequences

What are the implications of this issue for the stakeholders?

Question/Issue/Problem

How would a nuclear plant emergency affect the community?

Experienc/Evidence/Data

Research how the local nuclear power plant plans for emergencies. What future research is planned in this area? What are the arguments that stakeholder groups give for and against the nuclear energy provider's response plan?

Inferences

After gathering data about the response plan for nuclear power plant emergencies in your area, describe what this involves for students in your school. Discuss and evaluate the arguments for and against the response plan. On what data are the stakeholders' arguments based? Have you changed your point of view after hearing the arguments and reading the facts? Explain.

Concepts/Ideas

How can a scientific system be productive or dysfunctional? How are these ways evident when considering the nuclear power plant's response to emergencies?

Assumptions

What assumptions emerge related to this issue? What assumptions might major stakeholders in this issue hold? Why do you think so?

Adapted from Paul, R. (1992). *Critical Thinking: What every person needs to survive in a rapidly changing world.* Sonoma, CA: Foundation for Critical Thinking.

D. Research Model

The research model provides students with a way to approach an issue of significance and explore it individually or in small groups. Its organization follows the major elements of reasoning. Teachers are encouraged to model each stage of this process in class.

For specific, elaborated lessons for teaching the research model procure a copy of *A Guide to Teaching Research Skills and Strategies in Grades 4–12*, available for purchase from the Center for Gifted Education at The College of William and Mary.

The Research Model

1. **Identify your issue or problem.**

   What is the issue or problem?

   Who are the stakeholders and what are their positions?

   What is *your* position on this issue?

2. **Read about your issue and identify points of view or arguments through information sources.**

   What are my print sources?

   What are my media sources?

   What are my people sources?

   What primary and secondary source documents might I use?

   What are my preliminary findings based on a review of existing sources?

3. **Form a set of questions that can be answered by a specific set of data.** Examples:

   a. What would be the results of _____?

   b. Who would benefit and by how much?

   c. Who would be harmed and by how much?

   My research questions:

4. **Gather evidence through research techniques such as surveys, interviews, or analysis of primary and secondary source documents.**

   What survey questions should I ask?

   What interview questions should I ask?

   What generalizations do secondary sources give?

   What data and evidence can I find in primary sources to support different sides of the issue?

5. Manipulate and transform data so that it can be interpreted.

How can I summarize what I found out?

Should I develop charts, diagrams, or graphs to represent my data?

6. Draw conclusions and make inferences.

What do the data mean? How can I interpret what I found out?

How do the data support your original point of view?

How do they support other points of view?

What conclusions do you make about the issue?

7. Determine implications and consequences.

What are the consequences of following the point of view that you support?

Do I know enough or are there now new questions to be answered?

8. Communicate your findings. (Prepare an oral presentation for classmates based on note cards and written report.)

What are my purpose, issue, and point of view, and how will I explain them?

What data will I use to support my point of view?

How will I conclude my presentation?

4. Data Table Construction

Scientists communicate information through many methods including organizational tools such as data tables. Designing data tables should be part of all students' experiences so that they can organize and communicate their findings clearly prior to drawing inferences from their collected data. *The National Science Education Standards* emphasize interpretation of data collected by students as early as the fourth grade. Younger students may be initially more comfortable with precollected sets of data.

Data refers to the measurements made when conducting experiments. Measurements of speed, distance, and temperature are examples of data. By organizing data into tables, the scientist can see patterns in the results.

In constructing data tables, there are some common conventions for facilitating communication between the writer and reader. For example, the independent variable is recorded in the left column and the dependent variable is recorded in the right column. Also, when repeated trials are conducted, the column for the dependent variable is divided into smaller columns so that data can be recorded for each repeated trial.

Title:				
Independent Variable	**Dependent Variable**			**Average Measurement/Observation**
	Trials			

Title The purpose of the experiment should be included in the title.

Independent variable The independent variable should be clearly stated. This is the variable that is purposefully changed.

Dependent variable The dependent variable should be clearly stated. If repeated trials are to be run, the columns under the dependent variable should be divided according to the number of trials run by the experimenter. This is the variable affected by the independent variable.

Average measurement The average measurement and unit of measure should be listed, if applicable. Measurements should be organized either into ascending or descending order.

Rezba, R. J., Sprague, C., Fiel, R. L. (2003). *Learning and assessing science process skills* (4th ed.). Dubuque, IA: Kendall/Hunt Publishing Company.

4

Appendices

The Concept of Systems

A

The Concept of Systems

(Taken from *Guide to Teaching a Problem-Based Science Curriculum,* Center for Gifted Education, 1997)

A system is a collection of things and processes that interact with each other and together constitute a meaningful whole. Examples from the realm of science include atoms, chemical reaction systems, individual cells, organs, organ systems, organisms, ecosystems, solar systems, and galaxies; nonscience examples include sewer systems, political systems, the banking system, transportation systems, and so on. All systems share certain properties:

1. Systems have identifiable elements.
2. Systems have definable boundaries.
3. Most systems receive input in the form of materials or information from outside their boundaries and generate output to the world outside their boundaries.
4. The interactions of system elements with each other and their response to input from outside the system combine to determine the overall nature and behavior of the system.

Systems are made up of identifiable elements and processes. The elements comprising an ecosystem, for example, include all of the organisms present as well as all of the physical features of the bushes and smaller plants; the insects, birds, and other animals present; the nature of the terrain; the quality of the soil; the availability of water; the weather; and so on. Defining the elements of an ecosystem thoroughly is a large task. Similarly, the elements of nonscience systems are clearly definable. A school system would include all of the physical property appertaining to the schools and their administration: schools, playgrounds, buses, administration buildings, and so on. It also includes all of the teachers, pupils, administrators, and (ideally) parents.

The boundaries of systems must also be defined. The boundaries of an ecosystem are defined physically; they are the boundaries of the territory that it occupies. Thus, the boundary of a forest ecosystem is the edge of the forest. An ecosystem's boundaries can be drawn somewhat arbitrarily; one can speak of a backyard ecosystem or of the planetary ecosystem. The first ecosystem would thus be an element of the second ecosystem. The appropriate choice of boundaries for an ecosystem depend on the phenomena that one wishes to study: to study global warming, it is necessary to include the whole planet, but a study of the effects of man on the alpine tundra could involve only a single mountaintop. Similarly, the boundaries of nonscience systems can be defined in somewhat arbitrary ways depending on the nature of the process under study. The boundaries of a school system could be chosen to exclude neighboring systems and the federal government: although all of these elements can affect the school system, they are not really integral to its behavior.

Drawing the boundaries of a system appropriately can reveal much about its nature and behavior. Including phenomena and elements that are irrelevant to the properties under study will make understanding the system unnecessarily difficult. Including detailed consideration of the daily actions of members of the Williamsburg City Council in a study of overall behavior of the American political system adds variables that are probably insignificant for the behavior of the system as a whole and therefore makes the study of the system unnecessarily difficult. Excluding the press from the system, however, probably decreases the understanding of the system, even though the press is not a formally defined branch of government. Although the press could be considered as an external factor that produces input into the system, in practice the actions of the press are so tightly intermeshed with the actions of those that run the government that excluding the press from the government system would make understanding the system more difficult rather than less.

As discussed in *Science for All Americans* (1990), one of the best examples of the importance of properly defining the boundaries and elements of an experimental system is Louis Pasteur's elegant experimental solution for the problem of the spontaneous generation of living organisms. Before the nineteenth century, it was widely believed that living organisms arose spontaneously from nonliving matter, without benefit of the action of other living things. Rats and mice were thought to arise spontaneously from old rags; maggots from old meat. In the 1800s, Louis Pasteur approached this problem experimentally and resolved it. He showed that if flies were kept from contact with meat, no maggots subsequently arose from old meat; and if meat broth was boiled and then kept in sealed flasks or in flasks that allowed the entry of air but not of dust particles, then the broth did not spoil. By drawing the boundaries of his experimental system to exclude certain elements (namely, flies and bacteria), Pasteur proved that meat alone was insufficient to generate maggots and meat broth alone did not spoil. Thus, the doctrine of spontaneous generation was laid to rest.

Another example of the importance of correctly understanding the boundaries and elements integral to a system comes from the controversy over the origin of life on Earth. The science of thermodynamics has been used (inappropriately) to argue that life could not have evolved from nonliving chemicals through simple life forms and up to the many complex forms that we see today; this argument is based on a misunderstanding of the boundaries of the system in which life evolved and an incomplete understanding of thermodynamics. Thermodynamics is the science that sets the limits on the energy efficiency and possible outcome of physical and chemical processes. The three laws of thermodynamics can be summarized as follows:

1. Energy can neither be created nor destroyed, only transferred or changed from one form to another.
2. In an irreversible process, the entropy (degree of disorder) of the universe increases; only in a reversible process will it stay constant. The entropy of the universe cannot decrease.
3. At the temperature absolute zero, the entropy of perfect crystals and compounds is zero.

The second law of thermodynamics has been misused to argue that life could not possibly have evolved, because over time the complexity of living things has increased, and hence the system of life on Earth has become more ordered, not more disordered. The basic flaw in this argument is that its proponents have neglected to include the sun in their calculations. Solar energy is the source of most of the energy used by organisms; thus, the thermodynamic properties of the sun must be included in the system. The net entropy of the sun has increased by a degree that is orders of magnitude greater than the degree of entropy decrease caused by the origin and actions of all life on Earth; thus, the entropy of the universe has increased, as it theoretically should.

A third fundamental property of systems is that they can receive input from and act on the world outside their boundaries. Input into a school system, for example, includes federal financial and material assistance. Output from a school system includes educated students. Input into an ecosystem includes such things as solar energy; output from an ecosystem includes such things as carbon dioxide released into the atmosphere as a result of animal respiration and oxygen released by plants.

The final fundamental property of a system is that its overall behavior depends on the properties and interactions of its parts. For example, understanding the behavior of an ecosystem (for example, whether it is stable or likely to change, whether it is delicate and sensitive to the incursions of man, or whether it can survive human influence with few changes) depends upon understanding the roles of the different elements in the ecosystem and their interactions. Thus, prediction of the number of deer that can be safely hunted in a given area depends upon knowing how fast they reproduce, which wild predators are present and what percentage of the deer population they kill, whether disease is present in the deer population and likely to reduce numbers substantially, which plants the deer used for food and how many deer the plant population can support without being reduced too far to replace itself, and so on.

This dependence of the behavior of the whole system on the properties and interactions of its parts is also seen in nonscience systems. The behavior of the federal government depends on the actions and motivations of its members, their interactions with each other, and their reactions to input from their constituents and from the outside world. The behavior of the local sewer system depends on the amount of material it receives, the age of the pipes, the capacity of the treatment plant, and so on. Attempting to understand the behavior of the whole system based on the nature of its parts is the essence of the philosophy of reductionism, which has been a highly successful approach to the study of systems in general.

Rationale for Teaching the Concept

The understanding of the behavior of one system will help understanding of other systems. Defining the elements, boundaries, inputs, and outputs of a system helps to understand its behavior as a whole. Once a child has learned to do this for a simple system, he or she will be able to apply the process to other, more complex systems. This will help him or her understand the scientific process, as setting up successful experiments involves determining which elements should be included and paying close attention to the inputs and outputs of the system; varying the elements present in the experimental system may well change the experimental outcome in ways that illuminate the functioning of the system. More generally, the study of certain scientific systems will deepen a child's understanding of the world around him or her. Every child should have some understanding of the ecosystem of which he or she is an element and the solar system in which he or she resides.

Suggested Applications

There are two different ways to approach the concept of systems with children. The first involves weaving it into the experimental work that they do in the course of their science studies. Defining the experimental system thoroughly and paying attention to the essential variables in the system and excluding the others from consideration are activities critical to any lab science course. The second approach to the concept involves teaching learners about some basic scientific systems. Many scientific systems are accessible to children, at least at a simple level. These include systems from many disciplines, including chemistry, geology, biology, and astronomy, as listed (albeit in incomplete fashion) following:

Biology

ecosystems

organ systems

organism: physiology, behavior

Chemistry

chemical reaction systems

Geology

Meteorology

weather systems

Astronomy

solar systems

galaxies

Earth-moon system

The planet Earth as a geological system: plate tectonics and its manifestations geologic change in mountain ranges, river systems, and the like

References

Judson, H. F. (1980). *The search for solutions.* NY: Holt, Rinehart, & Winston.

Rutherford, F. J., & Ahlgren, A. (1989). *Science for all Americans.* NY: Oxford University Press.

Suggested Mini-Lessons

B

Suggested Mini-Lessons

The following suggested mini-lessons may be topics for which the review of concepts is necessary for students to grasp the intent of the lessons in the unit more easily.

Lesson	Suggested Mini-Lesson	Mini-Lesson Online Links
Lesson 4A: An Inside Look at Nuclear Power Plants	This site includes a lesson plan about nuclear reactors and energy generation. The site has other lessons that could supplement this unit.	http://www.nrc.gov/reading-rm/basic-ref/teachers/unit3.html
Lesson 5: Nuclear Reactions	Destination Mars: This lesson explores the advantages and disadvantages of a fission-propulsion system.	http://media.nasaexplores.com/lessons/01-060/9-12_1.pdf
Lesson 8: Radioactive Decay and Half-Life	Radioactive Decay—A Sweet Simulation of a Half-Life: This lesson provides a simulation of radioactive decay.	http://www.sciencenetlinks.com/lessons.cfm?DocID=178
Lesson 10: Radiation Exposure	Teaching About Nature's Nuclear Reactors: This informational packet provides resources related to naturally occurring nuclear reactors.	http://arxiv.org/ftp/physics/papers/0507/0507088.pdf
Lesson 12: Shielding Experiment	Radiation Protection: How Much Is Enough? This lesson studies the effects of shielding on the amount of detectable radioactivity from a gamma source.	http://www.unt.edu/scope/Lesson%20Plans/Radioactivity/Radioactivity1.htm
Lesson 16: A Look at Chernobyl	Fallout from Chernobyl: This lesson plan examines the effect of a nuclear accident.	http://www.nationalgeographic.com/xpeditions/lessons/14/g68/fallout.html

Interdisciplinary Connections

C

Interdisciplinary Connections

These interdisciplinary connections activities may be used in a variety of ways. They may be:

- Assigned to students as extension activities;
- Used for enrichment purposes in classroom learning centers; or
- Included as supplementary activities for the unit.

Connecting to . . . *Mathematics*

- Use a graphing calculator to analyze half-life of a radioactive substance. Go to http://fcit.usf.edu/math/lessons/activities/HalfLifT.htm for lesson plans. Students will model a real-life condition by collecting data, graphing data, then using a graphing calculator to draw a "curve of best fit."

Connecting to . . . *Language Arts*

- Have students take on the role of the administrative manager of a nuclear power plant. Pose the scenario that there has been a "near accident" at the plant. The press will be arriving shortly for a press conference. Have students use the **Reasoning Model** to think through the situation and write a script for the press conference.

Connecting to . . . *Social Studies*

- Have students research the locations of nuclear power plants in the United States. Ask them to create a map illustrating the locations of these power plants. Using the **Reasoning Model,** ask students to think through the reasons for the locations, assumptions about nuclear power, and implications for the citizens.

Connecting to . . . *The Arts*

- Using the website http://www.infcty.net/, learn about Infinity City, a collaborative exhibition by artists Ann T. Rosenthal and Stephen Moore that explores life in the atomic age. Discuss art that is designed to raise awareness or make a political statement.
- Use the photos located at http://www.jeromegoolsby.net/nucflash/nuketoc.html to explore the elements of art: color, form, symmetry, texture, and so on.

Supplemental Readings for Students

D

Supplemental Readings for Students

Fiction	Nonfiction
Aunt Carrie's War Against Black Fox Nuclear Power Plant Carrie Barefoot Dickerson Stillwater, OK: Council Oak Distribution (1995) ISBN: 1571780092	*The Chain Reaction: Pioneers of Nuclear Science* Karen Fox Danbury, CT: Franklin Watts (2000) ISBN: 0531114252
The Bomb Theodore Taylor San Diego, CA: Harcourt & Brace (1995) ISBN: 0380727234	*The Chernobyl Disaster: April 26, 1986* Paul Dowswell Austin, TX: Steck-Vaughn (2004) ISBN: 0739860496
Downwind Louise Moeri New York: Random House ISBN-13: 9780525440963 Limited availability, out of print but available from used book sellers	*Chernobyl: Nuclear Disaster* Nichol Bryan New York: Gareth Stevens ISBN: 0836855043
The Far Side of Evil Sylvia Louise Engdahl New York: Walker (2003) ISBN: 0802788483	*Meltdown: A Race Against Nuclear Disaster at Three Mile Island* Wilborn Hampton New York: Candlewick Press (2001) ISBN: 0763607150
Phoenix Rising Karen Hesse New York: Puffin Books (1995) ISBN: 0140376283	*Nuclear Energy: Troubled Past, Uncertain Future* Laurence Pringle NY: Simon & Schuster Childrens Publishing ISBN: 0027753913
Tracking Bear Aimee Thurlo and David Thurlo New York: Forge (2003) ISBN: 0765343967	*Nuclear Power: Promise or Peril?* Michael J. Daley Minneapolis: Lerner Publications (1997) ISBN: 0822526115
	Powerhouse: Inside a Nuclear Power Plant Charlotte Wilcox and Jerry Boucher Lerner Publishing Group Minneapolis, MN: ISBN: 087614945X
	The Radioactive Boy Scout Ken Silverstein New York: Random House (2004) ISBN: 037550351X

Suggested Rubrics

E

The rubrics provided in this section may be used for assessment purposes when teaching the unit. The rubrics include:

- Experimental Design Rubric
- Connections to Systems Concept Rubric
- Oral Presentation Rubric
- Persuasive Writing Rubric

A source of rubrics for use specifically in the science classroom is:

Lantz, H. B. (2004). *Rubrics for assessing student achievement in science grades K–12*. Thousand Oaks, CA: Corwin Press, Inc.

Experimental Design Rubric

Criteria	Strong Evidence 2	Some Evidence 1	No Evidence 0	Pre	Post
States **PROBLEM** or **QUESTION**.	Clearly states the problem or question to be addressed.	Somewhat states the problem or question to be addressed.	Does not state the problem or question to be addressed.		
Generates a **PREDICTION** and/or **HYPOTHESIS**.	Clearly generates a prediction or hypothesis appropriate to the experiment.	Somewhat generates a prediction or hypothesis appropriate to the experiment.	Does not generate a prediction or hypothesis.		
Lists experiment steps.	Clearly & concisely lists four or more steps as appropriate for the experiment design.	Clearly & concisely lists one to three steps as appropriate for the experiment design.	Does not generate experiment steps.		
Arranges steps in **SEQUENTIAL** order.	Lists experiment steps in sequential order.	Generally lists experiment steps in sequential order.	Does not list experiment steps in a logical order.		
Lists **MATERIALS** needed.	Provides an inclusive and appropriate list of materials.	Provides a partial list of materials needed.	Does not provide a list of materials needed.		
Plans to **REPEAT TESTING** and tells reason.	Clearly states a plan to conduct multiple trials, providing reasoning.	Clearly states a plan to conduct multiple trials.	Does not state plan or reason to repeat testing.		
DEFINES the terms of the experiment.	Correctly defines all relevant terms of the experiment.	Correctly defines some of the relevant terms of the experiment.	Does not define terms, or defines terms incorrectly.		
Plans to **MEASURE**.	Clearly identifies plan to measure data.	Provides some evidence of planning to measure data.	Does not identify plan to measure data.		
Plans **DATA COLLECTION**.	Clearly states plan for data collection, including note-taking, the creation of graphs or tables, etc.	States a partial plan for data collection.	Does not identify a plan for data collection.		
States plan for **INTERPRETING DATA**.	Clearly states plan for interpreting data by comparing data, looking for patterns and reviewing previously known information.	States a partial plan for interpreting data.	Does not state plan for interpreting data.		
States plan for drawing a **CONCLUSION BASED ON DATA**.	Clearly states plan for drawing conclusions based on data.	States a partial plan for drawing conclusions based on data.	Does not state plan for drawing conclusions.		

TOTAL SCORE:

Adapted from Fowler, M. (1990). The diet cola test. *Science Scope, 13(4)*, 32–34.

Connections to Systems Concept Rubric

Target Skills	Novice	Developing	Proficient	Exemplary
Connection to Systems Concept	• Student has little or no knowledge of systems vocabulary.	• Student exhibits knowledge of systems vocabulary.	• Student attempts to use systems vocabulary; the use is sometimes inaccurate.	• Student uses systems vocabulary accurately.
	• Student treats the concept of systems and scientific processes separately.	• Student recognizes links between the concept of systems and scientific processes.	• Student links the concept of systems with scientific processes.	• Student links the concept of systems and scientific processes in novel ways.
	• Student makes no connection between the problem resolution and the concept of systems.	• Student demonstrates limited ability to connect problem resolution with the concept of systems.	• Student demonstrates the ability to connect problem resolution with the concept of systems.	• Student recognizes problem resolution and systems connections beyond the scope of the unit problem.

Oral Presentation Rubric

Target Skills	Novice	Developing	Proficient	Exemplary
Oral Communication Skills	• The speaker's purpose is unclear.	• The speaker's purpose needs additional clarification.	• The speaker's purpose is clear.	• The speaker's purpose is clear and fully developed.
	• Student maintains little or no eye contact with audience.	• Student sometimes maintains eye contact with audience.	• Student mostly maintains appropriate eye contact with audience.	• Student consistently maintains appropriate eye contact with audience.
	• Student articulation is unclear and difficult to understand.	• Student articulation is generally clear but may not always be correct.	• Student articulates clearly and correctly.	• Student articulates clearly, correctly, and precisely.
	• Student does not use appropriate volume.	• Student is sometimes difficult to hear.	• Student uses appropriate volume most of the time.	• Student uses appropriate volume and considers audience size and room capacity.

continued

Oral Presentation Rubric (Continued)

Target Skills	Novice	Developing	Proficient	Exemplary
Oral Communication Skills (continued)	• Distracters in language and body movement overwhelm the presentation.	• Minimal distracters in language and body movement are present.	• Distracters in language and body movement are absent.	• Students uses language and body movement to enhance, not distract from, the presentation.
	• Student word choice is inappropriate and imprecise.	• Student word choice is inappropriate or imprecise.	• Student word choice is appropriate and precise.	• Student word choice is precise and sophisticated.
Organization Skills	• Little organization is evident in the presentation.	• Limited organization is evident in the presentation.	• Information is presented in an organized sequence.	• Information is presented in an organized and engaging sequence.
	• The presentation shows little evidence of planning.	• The presentation shows some evidence of planning.	• The presentation shows thoughtful planning.	• The presentation shows thoughtful planning and careful construction.
Visual Display Skills	• Visual aids detract from the presentation.	• Visual aids are not appropriately incorporated into the presentation.	• Visual aids complement presentation information.	• Visual aids enhance and reinforce presentation information.
Problem Resolution Skills	• The problem resolution does not consider stakeholder perspectives.	• The problem resolution makes some reference to stakeholder perspectives.	• The problem resolution considers a limited number of stakeholder perspectives.	• The problem resolution considers multiple stakeholder perspectives.
	• There is no connection made between the problem resolution and the information discovered through research.	• Some connection is made between the problem resolution and the information discovered through research.	• Obvious connections are made between the problem resolution and information discovered through research.	• Sophisticated connections are made between the problem resolution and information discovered through research.

Persuasive Writing Scoring Rubric

Claim or Opinion

0   No clear position exists on the writer's assertion, preference, or view, and context does not help to clarify it.

2   Yes or no (alone), or writer's position is poorly formulated but reader is reasonably sure what the paper is about based on context.

4   *Meets expectations:* A clear topic sentence exists, and the reader is reasonably sure what the paper is about based on the strength of the topic sentence alone.

6   *Exceeds expectations:* A very clear, concise position is given and position is elaborated with reference to reasons; multiple sentences are used to form the claim. Must include details that explain the context.

Data or Supporting Points

0   No reasons are offered that are relevant to the claim.

2   One or two weak reasons are offered; the reasons are relevant to the claim.

4   At least two strong reasons are offered that are relevant to the claim.

6   *Meets expectations:* At least three reasons are offered that are relevant to the claim.

8   *Exceeds expectations:* At least three reasons are offered that are also accurate, convincing, and distinct.

Elaboration

0   No elaboration is provided.

2   An attempt is made to elaborate on at least one reason.

4   More than one reason is supported with relevant details.

6   *Meets expectations:* Each reason (three) is supported with relevant information that is clearly connected to the claim.

8   *Exceeds expectations:* The writer explains all reasons in a very effective, convincing, multiparagraph structure.

Conclusion

0   No conclusion or closing sentence is provided.

2   A conclusion or closing sentence is provided.

4   *Meets expectations:* A conclusion is provided that revisits the main ideas.

6   *Exceeds expectations:* A strong concluding paragraph is provided that revisits and summarizes main ideas.

5

References
and Resources

References

Aftergood, S., Hafemeister, D. W., Prilutsky, O. F., J.R. & Rodionov, S. N. (1991). Nuclear power in space. *Scientific American,* June, 42–47

Asimov, I. (1965). *New intelligent man's guide to science: The physical sciences.* NY: Basic Books.

Barrows, H. S. (1988). *The tutorial process.* Springfield, IL: Southern Illinois University School of Medicine.

Byrne, J., Crossett, B., & Bailey, B. (1990). *Tracking down thinking skills: A four-phase model for developing research processes.* National Association for Gifted Children Annual Convention, Little Rock, AR.

Caplan, R. (1990). *Our earth, ourselves.* NY: Bantam Books.

Center for Gifted Education (1997). *Guide to teaching a problem-based curriculum for high-ability learners.* Dubuque, IA: Kendall/Hunt Publishing Company.

Cothron, J. H., Giese, R. N., & Rezba, R. J. (2004a). *Science experiments by the hundreds* (2nd ed.). Dubuque, IA: Kendall/Hunt Publishing Company.

———. (2004b). *Science experiments by the hundreds: Teacher's guide* (2nd ed.). Dubuque, IA: Kendall/Hunt Publishing Company.

———. (2006a). *Science experiments and projects for students: Student version of students and research* (4th ed.). Dubuque, IA: Kendall/Hunt Publishing Company.

———. (2006b). *Students and research: Practical strategies for science classrooms and competitions* (4th ed.). Dubuque, IA: Kendall/Hunt Publishing Company.

Cramer, J., McCarroll, T., & McDowell, H. (1991). Time to choose. *Time,* April 29, 54–61.

Fermi, L. (1954). *Atoms in the family.* Chicago: University of Chicago Press.

Gofman, J. W. (1979). *An irreverent, illustrated view of nuclear power.* San Francisco, CA: Committee for Nuclear Responsibility.

Gould, J. M., & Goldman, B. A. (1991). *Deadly deceit.* NY: Four Walls Eight Windows.

Haber-Schain, V., Dogd, J. H., & Walter, J. A. (1986). *PSSC physics.* Lexington, MA: D. C. Heath & Company.

Hecht, M. M. (1991). Cold fusion: Good research, bad press. *21st Century Science and Technology,* 16–34.

Holt, Rinehart, & Winston. (1975) *Project physics.* NY: Holt, Rinehart, & Winston, Inc.

Kleg, M., & Totten, S. (1990a). Horizontal nuclear proliferation: Concepts, issues, and controversies. *Social Education,* March, 133–135.

———. (1990b). On teaching horizontal nuclear proliferation: A conceptual framework. *Social Education,* March, 136–142.

Levoy, G. (1988). Nukebusters. *Omni,* May, 14.

Loventhal, P. (1990). The nuclear power and nuclear weapons connection. *Social Education,* March, 146–150.

Martocci, B., & Wilson, G. *A basic guide to nuclear power.* Washington, DC: Edison Electric Institute.

Molander, R., & Nichols, R. (1985). *Who will stop the bomb?* NY: Facts on File.

Naar, J. (1990). *Design for a livable planet.* NY: Harper & Row Publishers.

Nair, D. (1987). Chernobyl: Asking the right questions. *The Science Teacher,* November, 25–33.

Nelkin, D. (1987). *Selling science: How the press covers science and technology.* NY: W.H. Freeman & Company.

Parisi, L., (Ed.) (1989). *Hot rods: Storage of spent nuclear fuel.* Boulder, CO: Social Science Education Consortium, Inc.

Pedersen, A. (1991). *Environment book.* Santa Fe, NM: John Muir Publications.

Piasecki, B., & Asmus, P. (1990). *In search of environmental excellence: Moving beyond blame.* NY: Simon & Schuster, Inc.

Radlauer, E., & Radlauer, R. (1985). *Nuclear tech talk*. Chicago: Children's Press.

Rathjens, G., & Miller, M. (1991). Nuclear proliferation after the cold war. *Technology Review,* August/September, 25–32.

Rezba, R. J., Sprague, C., & Fiel, R. L. (2003). *Learning and assessing science process skills* (4th ed.). Dubuque, IA: Kendall/Hunt Publishing Company.

Roberts, L. (1991). The geopolitics of nuclear waste. *Science* 251, February, 864–867.

Stepien, W. J., & Senn, P. R. (2000). *The internet and problem-based learning: Developing solutions through the Web.* Tucson, AZ: Zephyr Press.

Torp, L., & Sage, S. (2002). *Problems as possibilities: Problem-based learning for K–16 education* (2nd ed.). Thousand Oaks, CA

Weaver, K. F. (1981). Our energy predicament. *National Geographic,* February, 2–23.

Willis, J. (1988). *Earthlets as explained by Professor Xargle.* NY: E. P. Dutton.

Resources

Resource Books for Teachers

Andryszewski, Tricia. (1995). *What to do with nuclear waste.* Brookfield, CT: Millbrook.

Cole, Michael D. (2002). *Three Mile Island: Nuclear disaster.* Berkeley Heights, NJ: Enslow. (Series: American Disasters)

Condon, Judith. (1999). *Chernobyl and other nuclear accidents.* Austin, TX: Raintree Steck-Vaughn.

Cothran, Helen. Ed., (2002). *Energy alternatives: Opposing viewpoints.* San Diego, CA: Greenhaven Press.

Dowswell, Paul. (2004) *The Chernobyl disaster.* Austin, TX: Raintree Steck-Vaughn. (Series: Days That Shook the World)

Goldstein, Natalie. (2001). *How do we know the nature of the atom?* New York: Rosen. (Series: Great Scientific Questions and the Scientists Who Answered Them)

Hampton, Wilborn. (2001). *Meltdown: A race against nuclear disaster at Three Mile Island.* Cambridge, MA: Candlewick.

Knapp, Brian. (1996). *Uranium and other radioactive elements.* Danbury, CT: Grolier Educational. (Series: Elements)

Nardo, Don. (2002). *Atoms.* San Diego, CA: Kid Haven. (Series: Kid Haven Science Library)

U.S. Department of Energy. (ND). *Inventory of power plants in the United States.* [prepared by the Division of Electric Power Statistics, Office of Coal and Electric Power Statistics, Energy Information Administration, Department of Energy]. Washington, D.C.: U.S. Dept. of Energy, Energy Information Administration, Assistant Administrator for Energy Data Operations, Office of Coal and Electric Power Statistics: Available from the Supt. of Docs., U.S. G.P.O.

Wilcox, Charlotte. (1996). *Powerhouse: Inside a nuclear power plant.* Minneapolis, MN: Carolrhoda.

Winkler, Kathy. (1996). *Radiology.* New York: Benchmark. (Series: Inventors and Inventions).

Videos/DVDs

Meltdown at Three Mile Island (videorecording). 1999. A Steward/Gazit Productions, Inc., film for The American Experience (WGBH Boston); written and produced by Chana Gazit; co-produced and edited by David Steward. Alexandria, VA: PBS Home Video.

Chernobyl: A chronicle of difficult weeks. Directed by Vladmir Shevchenko. The first film made after the accident. This is a Russian documentary film with English subtitles. Available on VHS. See http://www.videoproject.net or call 1-800-4PLANET.

Meltdown. Experts explore technical causes behind three major nuclear accidents. Available on VHS or DVD. See http://www.films.com or call 1-800-257-5126.

BBC: Chernobyl: Ten days for disaster. A BBC documentary returning to the site 3 years after the accident. Available on VHS or DVD. See http://www.films.com or call 1-800-257-5126.

The Standard Deviants: The Dangerous World of Pre-Calculus Part 2. Contains a section on nuclear half-lives. Available on VHS. See http://www.standarddeviants.com or call 1-800-613-0368.

EME: Radiation and Environment. Introduction to radiation concepts, uses, and dangers. Available on VHS. See http://www.emescience.com or call 1-800-848-2050.

Websites

Chernobyl Children's Project International

This site offers facts about the 1986 disaster and gives information on efforts of humanitarian and medical aid.

http://www.ccp-intl.org/mission.html

The Energy Story

This award-winning website has a plethora of information on energy, its sources, uses and conservation. It also contains extensive resources for teachers and students about the many facets of energy.

http://www.energyquest.ca.gov

International Atomic Energy Authority

This site includes "Nuclear Power Plant Simulators for Education." These are educational simulators that simulate responses of water-cooled nuclear reactor types to operating and accident conditions.

http://www.iaea.org/programmes/ne/nenp/nptds/newweb2001/simulators/index.htm

Kids' Zone—Energy: Nuclear World

This Canadian interactive site for kids discusses the atom, uranium, fission, and spinoffs through color, text, and animation.

http://www.aecl.ca/kidszone/atomicenergy/nuclear/index.asp

Nuclear Energy Institute

This website offers a map of the United States showing which states have nuclear power plants. Additional links discuss nuclear technology, nuclear data, public policy issues, a library, safety and security issues, nuclear waste disposal, and transportation safety.

http://www.nei.org

Nuclear Power in Seaside: A WebQuest

In this WebQuest, students acting as specialists must create a special report to present at a town meeting of Seaside residents to help them determine whether or not to allow construction of a nuclear power plant.

http://powayusd.sdcoe.k12.ca.us/projects/NUKEWEB/default.htm

Nuclear Regulatory Commission

The Nuclear Regulatory Commission formulates policies and develops regulations governing nuclear reactor and nuclear material safety. Many resources are available on this website for use as background information and for resource purposes.
http://www.nrc.gov

Nuclear Regulatory Commission: Lesson Plans for Teachers

This site features five instructional units on nuclear-related subjects.
http://www.nrc.gov/reading-rm/basic-ref/teachers.html

Nuclear Regulatory Commission: Students' Corner

This site is designed for student use and features information about nuclear energy.
http://www.nrc.gov/reading-rm/basic-ref/students.html

The Problem of Nuclear Waste Disposal

This is part of a 1999 University of Oregon lecture series that includes U.S. Policy for waste disposal, additional Internet resources, and a list of what other countries are doing. Methods of burial (with diagram) and other possibilities are considered.
http://zebu.uoregon.edu/1999/ph161/l19.html

RadWaste.Org

This is a guide to radioactive waste, and nuclear, and radiation related material on the Internet.
http://www.radwaste.org/index.html

TVA Kids: Nuclear Power

This site, developed by the Tennessee Valley Authority, offers an explanation of power sources. A nuclear power link leads to "How Nuclear Power Works," which shows photographs and animated diagrams to explain uranium, fission, the inside of a nuclear power plant, and so on.
http://www.tvakids.com/electricity/nuclear.htm

U.S. Dept. of Energy

This site, a service of the Energy Information Administration (EIA), provides students, educators, and other users information about free and low-cost energy-related educational materials.
http://www.eia.doe.gov/bookshelf/eer/kiddietoc.html

The Virtual Nuclear Tourist!

This website offers an introduction and Frequently Asked Questions (FAQ) about power plants. There is a section on hot topics, a trip inside a nuclear power plant with many illustrations and diagrams both from the United States and world locations, and a daily plant status report.
http://www.nucleartourist.com/

Modular Units That May Be Integrated with *Nuclear Energy: Friend or Foe?*

- Hazardous Materials Investigations: The Barrel Mystery
- Waste Disposal: Computers and the Environment
  Developed by:
  SEPUP, Lawrence Hall of Science
  Distributed by:
  Lab-Aids, Inc.
  17 Colt Court
  Ronkonkoma, NY 11779
  Tel: 800-381-8003
  Fax: 631-737-1286
  http://www.sepup.com

Index